A Pictorial History
of
Harbor City Volunteer Ambulance Squad

A Pictorial History
of
Harbor City Volunteer Ambulance Squad

Melbourne, Florida 1966-1999

Sharon C. Irvin, Editor

Library of Congress Control Number: 2020903106
ISBN: Hardcover   978-1-7960-8834-2
               Softcover   978-1-7960-8835-9
               eBook   978-1-7960-8955-4

Print information available on the last page.

Rev. date: 02/24/2020

To order additional copies of this book, contact:
Xlibris
1-888-795-4274
www.Xlibris.com
Orders@Xlibris.com
805277

Table of Contents

Foreword

When the federal government increased the minimum wage in 1966, funeral homes in Brevard County felt they could no longer afford to provide emergency medical services. As a result, the southern end of the county was left without prompt emergency care and transportation. This crisis came to the attention of the public when in April of 1966 a young girl was struck by a car and seriously injured while crossing US 1 in Eau Gallie. The child lay in the road for 45 minutes before an ambulance from Central Brevard transported her to a nearby hospital. A few days after this incident, a group of seven concerned citizens gathered around a kitchen table at the home of Ed Franckewich. Thus HCVAS began and served South Brevard for 33 years until its dissolution on September 30, 1999.

Acknowledgements

This book was put together as a way of helping members give some closure to HCVAS while at the same time informing the community of its history. The people pictured in this book represent only a few of the many who were a part of HCVAS.

The material in this book was compiled from HCVAS archives, private collections, *Volunteer Vitals* (the HCVAS newsletter), and articles from newspapers and journals. We are indebted to Julia Irvin and Robert Taylor for their encouragement and review of the manuscript and to Nicole Hoier for her skills in converting video frames to stills.

The following people provided information and/or pictures to make the squad's history complete: Rick and Pam Bridges, Ed Dunson, Bill Hoskovec, Mike Hunt, Edith Koelsch, Mike LeBelle, Diane McCauley, Sue McCuiston, Jane Meier, Kevin Nelson, Ken Olivier, Joel and Linda Ostroff, Louise Owens, Scott and Sandy Penrod, Scott Schein, Dave Segona, Jim and Barbara Skidmore, and Les Williams. Special thanks goes to Thom Sousa, who as acting CEO approved the creation of this book and allocated the funds for its publication.

I.

Beginnings and Challenges 1966-1974

1. Three early HCVAS ambulances, including two vintage Cadillacs (one bought for $125), parked at 481 North Harbor City Boulevard in Melbourne. In 1966, Charles Roberts, a local M.D., rented the house to HCVAS for $1.00 a year to serve as the squad's first headquarters.

HARBOR CITY VOLUNTEER
AMBULANCE SQUAD
"CHARTER MEMBERS"

P — Ed E Franckewich Jr
V.P — Robert Michels
T — Robert Vicari Jr
TR — Michael Wiggins
TR — Homer Lewis
TR — Steve Stunich
S — Gene Lovett

James Stone

Chet Lambert
Tom Stuart
Horace Myers
Dick Levy
June Marie Michels
Dan Licata
Tom Wild
Barbara Lovett
Robert Sanborn
John Clarkson
Gene A Lewis

MEMBERS

Nancy Pearce
Geo Griggs

2. A list dated June 13, 1966 of HCVAS members. In April, seven concerned citizens (Ed Frankewich, Tom Wild, Gene Lovett, Robert Michels, Chet Lambert, Dick Levy, and John Clarkson) organized HCVAS to provide ambulance service to South Brevard (population 100,000). The squad, which was patterned after an established volunteer service in Mt. Holly, NJ, would not charge for its services nor have any paid employees. In June, it received a charter as a not-for-profit organization from Tom Adams, Florida Secretary of State.

3. Originally intended to be a back-up ambulance service, HCVAS
   eventually became the only full-time service in South Brevard.
   When dissolved on September 30, 1999, HCVAS served the
   area (see map) from Barnes Boulevard in Rockledge south to
   the Indian River County line (except for Barefoot Bay) and west
   to the Osceola County line.

4. Peggy Reardon and Billy Copeland standing in front of three HCVAS ambulances parked at the North Harbor City Boulevard headquarters (1966). John Clarkson, the Disaster Chief for Cape Kennedy and Patrick AFB, obtained donated equipment from missile contractors to stock four ambulances. County Commissioner Guy Brewster negotiated with Ed Franckewich, HCVAS president, to have the squad turn over the ambulance titles to the county in exchange for insurance coverage.

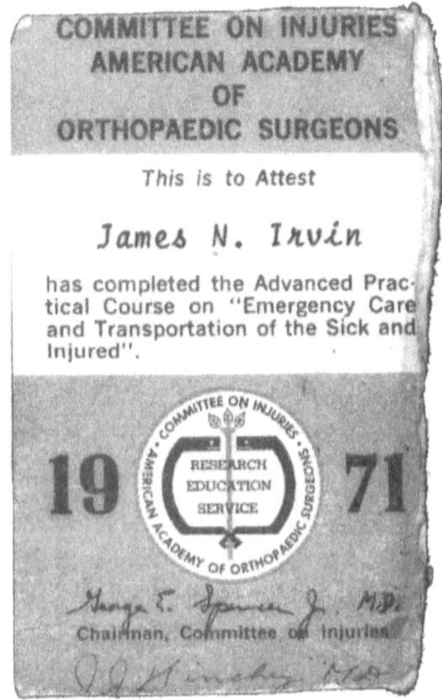

COMMITTEE ON INJURIES
AMERICAN ACADEMY
OF
ORTHOPAEDIC SURGEONS

This is to Attest

James N. Irvin

has completed the Advanced Practical Course on "Emergency Care and Transportation of the Sick and Injured".

19 71

Chairman, Committee on Injuries

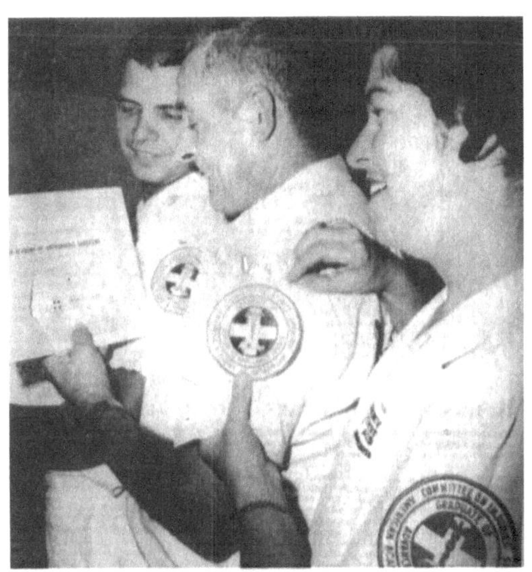

5. June Michels sewing an arm patch on John Clarkson's shirt as Chet Lambert checks his certificate (*The Daily Times*, 1966). In 1966 they went to Miami to attend the course *Emergency Care and Transportation of the Sick and Injured* conducted by the American Academy of Orthopedic Surgeons. The advanced course was taught at various colleges around the country from 1966 through 1971. Recipients received certificates designating them EMT-A (Ambulance). Also shown is Jim Irvin's 1971 certificate he received after attending the course at the University of Wisconsin, Madison.

6. A 1966 brochure explaining HCVAS' services to the community, including the availability of first aid classes.

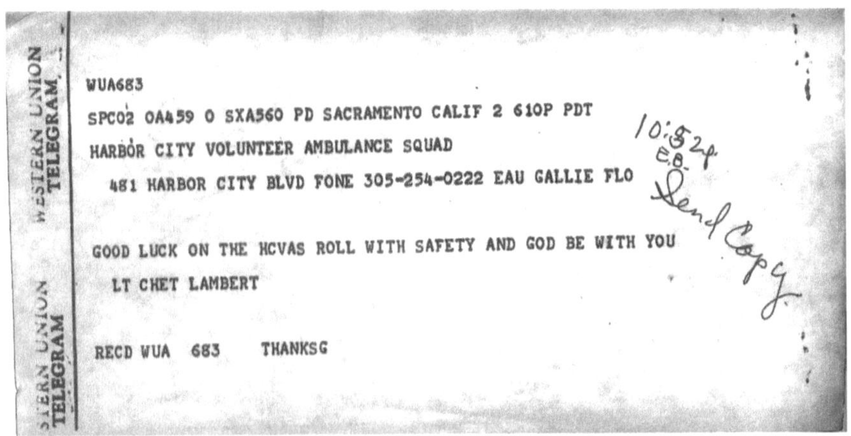

7.   A telegram sent to HCVAS on September 2, 1966 from Lt. Chet Lambert. Twenty-five volunteers had gone through rigorous training and drills to get certified in Red Cross Advanced First Aid. The squad began operating weekends and received its first call at 3:00 p.m. Labor Day. HCVAS' first patient was Frank Hyatt of Satellite Beach. On November 15, just 73 days later, 50 volunteers began operating the ambulance service 24 hours a day.

8.   An ad that appeared in *The South Brevard Shopping News*, inviting the community to HCVAS' open house on September 25, 1966.

Tri-City Volunteer Ambulance Team Announces October Calls, Services

As a public service to residents of Eau Gallie, Indian Harbour Beach and Satellite Beach, THE COURIER, in conjunction with Harbor City Volunteer Ambulance Squad, announces the following specifics of squad services performed during October:

	CALLS	MILES
Emergency	21	851
Drills	9	133
Service	11	95
Football games	8	84

There were a total of 49 calls, 1,163 miles traveled and 148 man-hours expended.

9. In November 1966, *The Courier* published a record of HCVAS' services performed in October.

THURSDAY - 1 DEC 66

	IN	OUT	
H. Forman	7/0530	1230	✓
T. A. McEntire	6:30/0600	1230	✓
H. Turner	8:30/8:30	5 oc	✓
I. Baxley	1:15/8:45	10 oc	✓
Jerry Baxley	1:35/1:30	6:05	✓
	4/400	1800	
DAN SCHAPPER	6/1800	HERE	✓
Leroy Water	6/6:00	1200	✓
JIM STONE	5:55/6.05	HERE	✓

Dispatchers
Jeanie Hughes	2:50/5:40	8:30
Cheryl Peacock	2:50/5:40	8:30
	5/	12:30
Timmy Adams	5/2:00	

10. A page dated December 1, 1966 from the first HCVAS volunteer
sign-in book.

11. A cartoon that appeared in the *Brevard Sentinel* on December 13, 1966. One of the biggest problems the volunteers faced was getting money to pay for equipment, maintenance, etc. The newspaper took the problem to the people, informing them of the benefits of a free ambulance service.

12. This cartoon asking for donations appeared in the *Orlando Sentinel* on February 9, 1967.

13. June Michels, John Clarkson, Jim Stone, Dick Levy, Bob Michels, and Chet Lambert celebrating HCVAS' 1st anniversary (*Florida Today*, June 14, 1967). In July, membership dwindled to 30 and the future looked gloomy for HCVAS. Possibly it would have to curtail its operations or go out of business. The newspaper saved the day by publishing an appeal for help. Within two weeks, HCVAS had a class of 154 new attendants with more applications coming in daily.

14. Mrs. Chester Lambert, Edith Koelsch and Jim Myers standing beside one of HCVAS' four ambulances (*Florida Today*, July 27, 1967). Some of the first ambulances bought by the squad had been stolen from up North and recovered by the Melbourne police. The owner of the ambulances elected to sell them to HCVAS rather than transport them back up North.

HARBOR CITY VOLUNTEER AMBULANCE SQUAD

481 Harbor City Blv'd

Eau Gallie, Florida

Two years ago a small child lay injured on one of our streets for 45 minutes waiting for an ambulance. The HARBOR CITY VOLUNTEER AMBULANCE SQUAD was formed to avert another tragedy such as this. Over the past two years, the Squad has grown to four ambulances and full time operations. Just recently, we have expanded our operations by placing an ambulance on the beach area from 6 P.M. to 6 A.M. When volunteers from the beach area have been properly trained, this ambulance will be available full time - 24 hours a day!

At the present time, we are answering an average of 3 calls per day. Some of these calls are being run to Miami, Gainesville and Orlando. In addition to giving emergency care and transportation to the sick and injured, the Squad also offers first aid instruction, provides ambulance for football games, auto races, air boat races, and any other special events we are requested to attend.

The HARBOR CITY VOLUNTEER AMBULANCE SQUAD is a non-profit organization. Therefore, we cannot charge for our services. The existence of this Squad depends entirely upon public donations. We solicit your support so that we can fulfill our motto: "HELP US TO HELP YOU." Your donations are tax deductible and appreciated.

If you can volunteer some of your time, we would appreciate your calling the Squad headquarters at 254- 6922. Both men and women are encouraged to join. Young adults between the ages of 16 and 21 are also needed as dispatchers.

THANK YOU FOR SUPPORTING US ! ! !

THE MEMBERS OF THE HARBOR CITY VOLUNTEER AMBULANCE SQUAD

15. A June 1968 press release explaining HCVAS' services, including coverage for football games and auto and air boat races. The squad now operated a roaming ambulance in North Indialantic from 6:00 p.m. to 6:00 a.m.

16. Jim Horner from RCA Corp. presenting June Michels and Dee Kovarik with a $300 check for the October 1968 fund-drive.

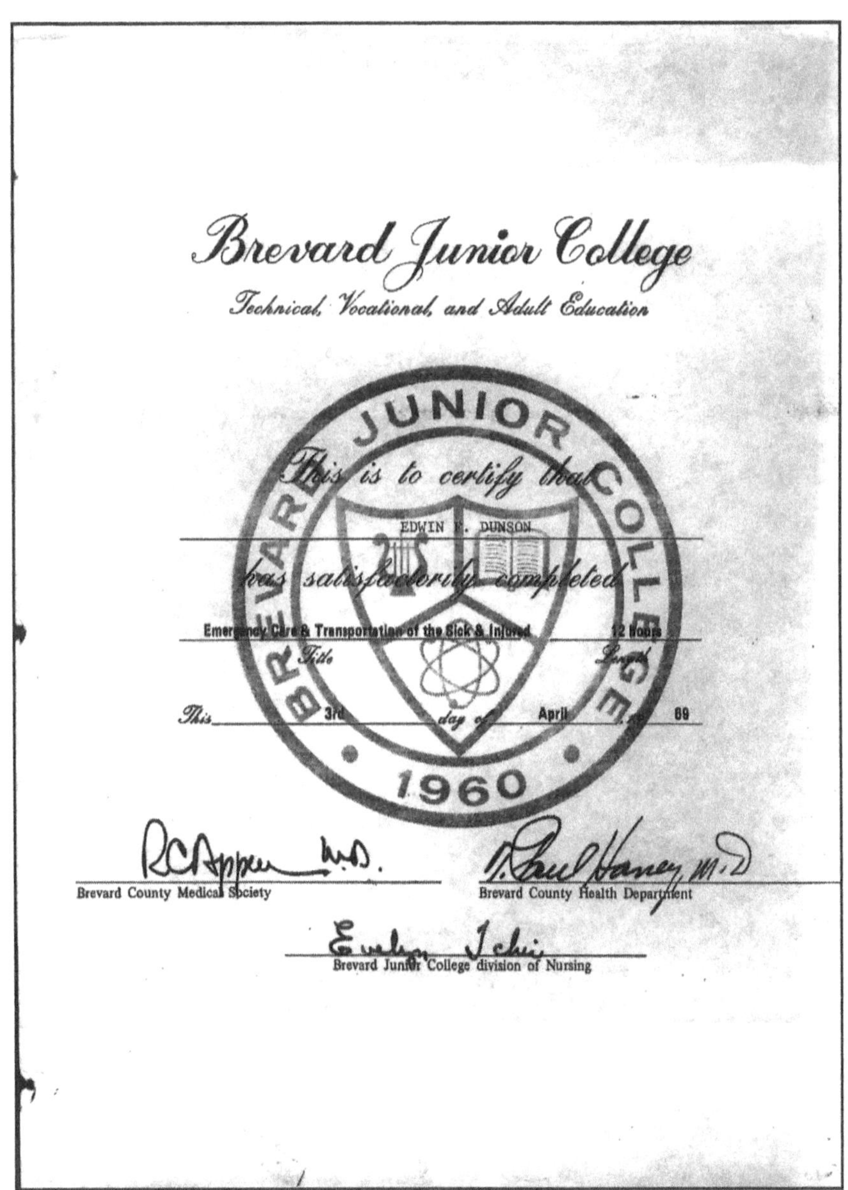

17. Edwin Dunson's certificate dated April 3, 1969. He had completed the course *Emergency Care & Transportation of the Sick & Injured* at Brevard Jr. College.

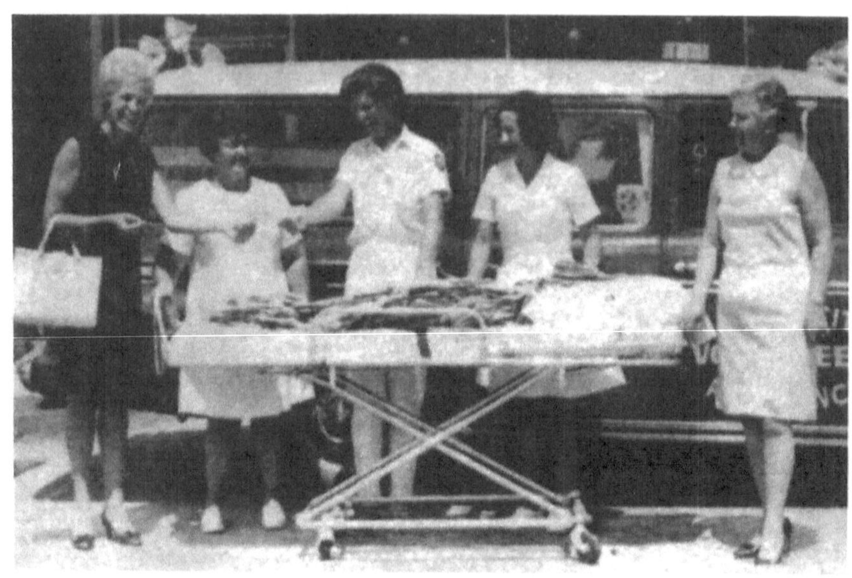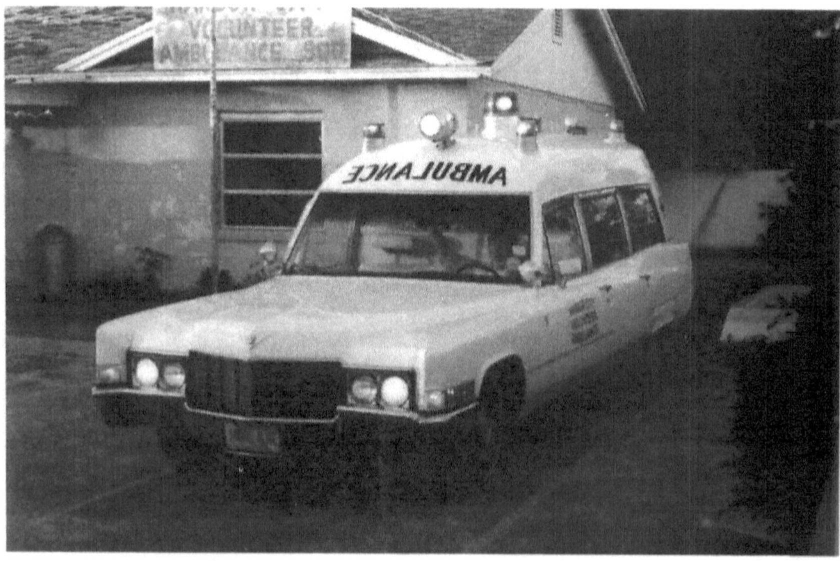

18. Edith Koelsch, Virgie Mustaine, and Vera Dunson cashing in 608½ books of S & H Green Stamps valued at $1,217 (*Daily Times*, May 29, 1969). The stamps were used towards the purchase of a $9,000 high-top Cadillac (Unit 9). Shown parked at the North Harbor City Boulevard headquarters, the ambulance was used primarily for long distance transports.

19. Judy Smith (17), Satellite High senior, dispatching at the N. Harbor City Blvd. headquarters (*Orlando Sentinel*, June 27, 1971). The original bylaws stated that members had to be at least 21 years of age. When the squad recognized the value of young people, the membership was divided into two categories: senior members (21 and over) and junior members (under 21). Junior members served as dispatchers until they were 18 when they were eligible to become ambulance attendants.

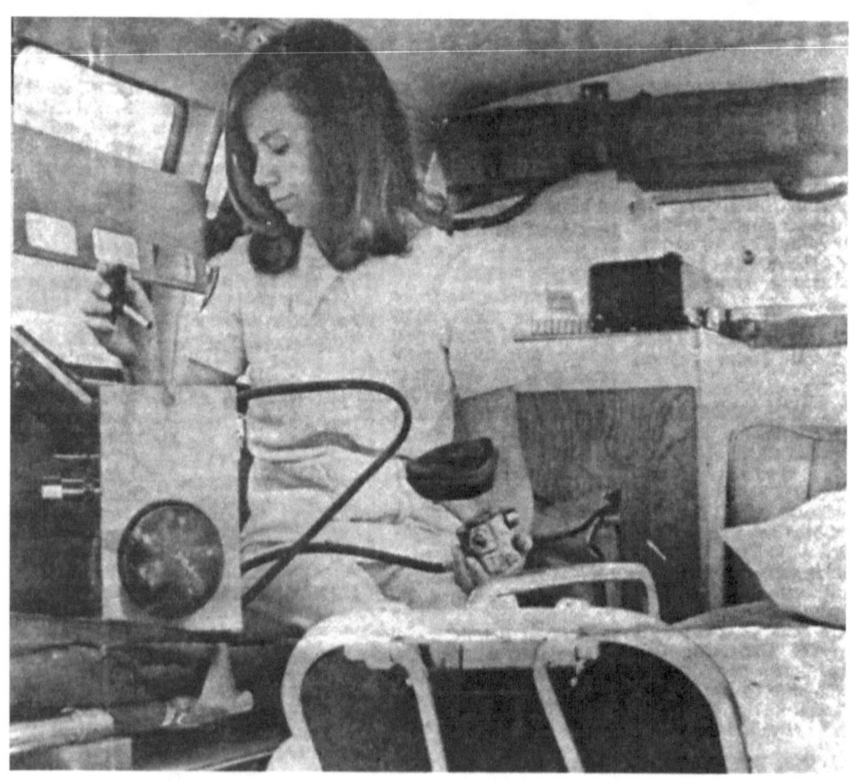

20. Judy Malnassy checking the portable oxygen before an ambulance call (*Orlando Sentinel*, June 27, 1971).

21. Shown next to Unit 2, HCVAS' first van, at headquarters on
North Harbor City Boulevard are:

Top left:
   Mark Plasner

Top right:
   Rick Bridges
   Bob Henderson
   Tony Lusich

Bottom left:
   Bill Booth
   Kitty Boone
   Pete Wells

Bottom right:
   Nick Gural
   Kitty Boone
   Mike Ussak (1972)

22. Unit 14, the Scuba Search & Rescue Unit (SSRU). In June 1972, a group of scuba divers at HCVAS felt the community needed a professional scuba search and rescue team. They obtained a surplus fire truck and converted it into a scuba emergency vehicle.

23. Linda Bragg ready for an ambulance call at the North Harbor City Boulevard headquarters (1973).

24. Members standing next to a conversion van (front row left to right): Louise Owens, Ricky Locklear, Ken Bragg, Linda Bragg, Linda Ostroff, Judy Smith, and Ken Olivier; (back row left to right): Tom Kender, Warren Wiley, Mark Plasner, Steve Ellis, and Harry Reineke. The standard uniform was white or navy pants with a white shirt and red jacket.

25. Unit 3 responding to a call from headquarters on North Harbor City Boulevard near Ballard Drive (1973).

26. A game of basketball at Florida Institute of Technology in January 1973: HCVAS vs. the Girls' Athletic Association. Shown playing are Jim Irvin and Scott Penrod.

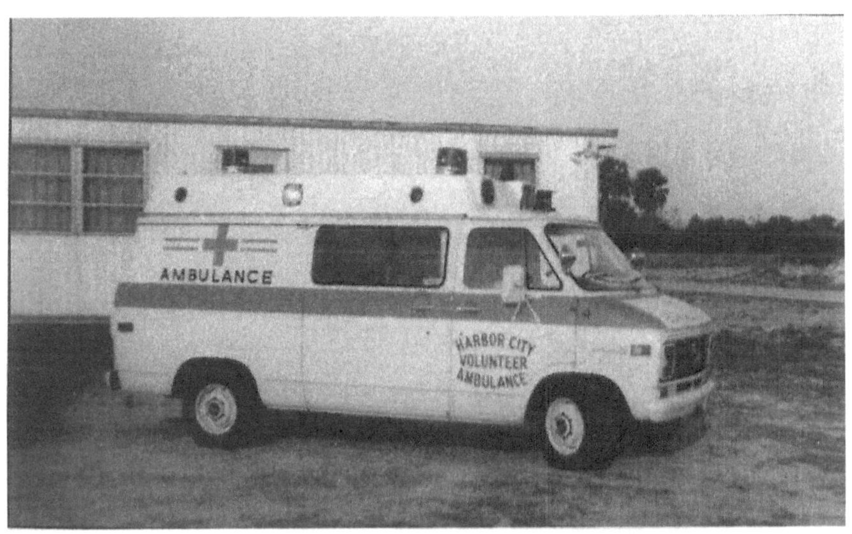

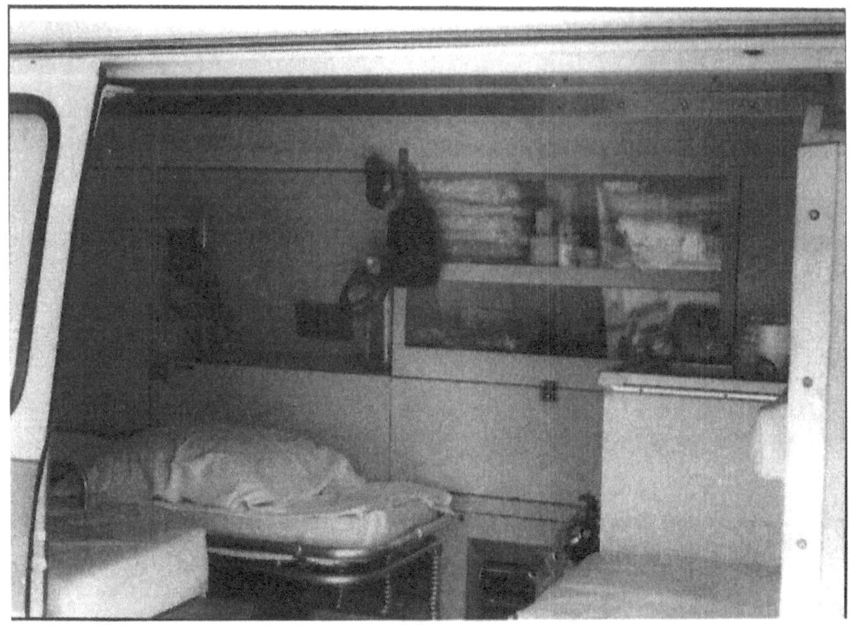

27. Unit 4 parked at HCVAS' first substation in Indialantic at Hoover Jr. High (1973). The beach community raised money to buy the mobile home. An inside look at the unit shows the main oxygen controls, suction, bag mask resuscitator, and storage area.

28. Connie Olivier dispatching at the North Harbor City Boulevard headquarters (1973). Dispatchers answered the phone, "Harbor City Volunteer Ambulance Squad, is this an emergency?"

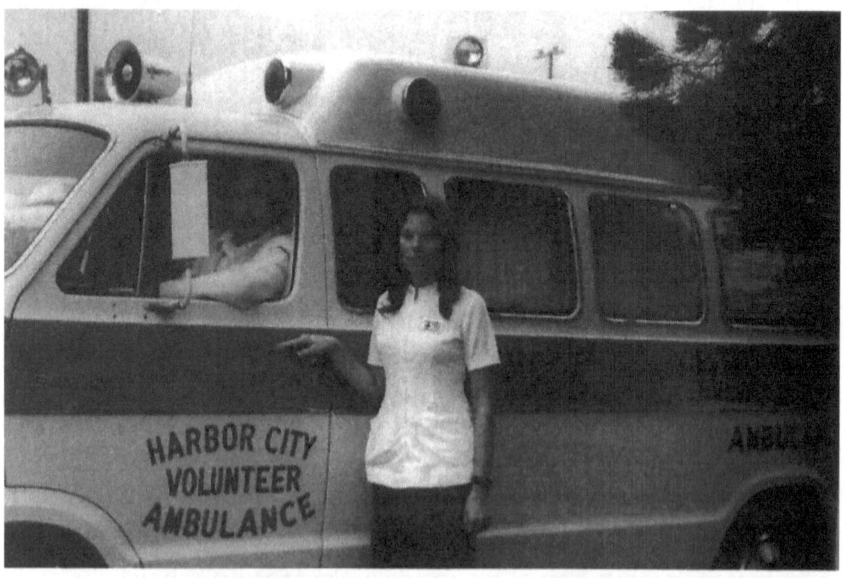

29. Karen and John Emond with Unit 5, a high top van, covering a special event at the Grant Seafood Fest (1973).

30. In 1973, the Melbourne Airport Authority donated a building at 530 Harvey Ogden Drive for HCVAS' second headquarters when the house on North Harbor City Boulevard was sold.

31. A business card that crews handed to family members assisted by HCVAS.

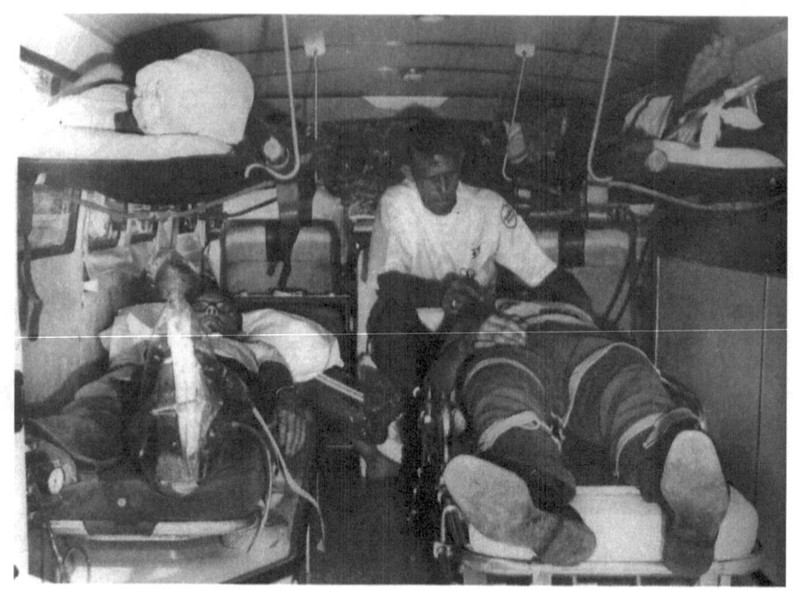

32. **Southern Ambulance** advertising its new ambulance (its cost was under $5,000). It could transport up to 5 patients at one time with 4 on stretchers (1973).

33. Some members including Terry McGovern playing touch football near the headquarters on Harvey Ogden Drive.

HARBOR CITY

VOLUNTEER AMBULANCE SQUAD, INC.
530 HARVEY OGDEN DRIVE
MELBOURNE, FLORIDA 32901

EMERGENCY TELEPHONE: 727-1444
BUSINESS TELEPHONE: 724-4411

"HELP US HELP YOU!"

The Eau Gallie Lions Club donated $1,000.00 to the Harbor City Volunteer Ambulance Squad Building Fund and issued a challenge to all other clubs to match their donation. The American Legion, Frank B. Huddleston, Post 81 Melbourne met and exceeded that challenge. Will your club be next???

"HELP US HELP YOU!" This is our plea to the people of South Brevard. Five dollars per family will reach our goal of $100,000.00. The headquarters building will be located on Hickory Street near Brevard Hospital on land donated by the City of Melbourne.

Remember this is South Brevard's ONLY ambulance service and there is never a fee charged for this service. YOUR ambulance service depends upon the generosity of its friends and supporters. Please mail your check today to P.O. Box 894, Melbourne, Florida 32935 or 530 Harvey Ogden Drive, Melbourne, Florida 32901.

Thank you,

Bob Johnson
Chairman
H.C.V.A.S. Building Fund

drt

Fund Balance 11/7/73 $35,000.00

34. This ad asking for donations appeared in the *Brevard Shopping News* on November 7, 1973. In September, HCVAS had started an 18-month fund drive to raise $100,000 for a permanent headquarters on Hickory Street in Melbourne. Since its inception in 1966, HCVAS had responded to 25,000 calls.

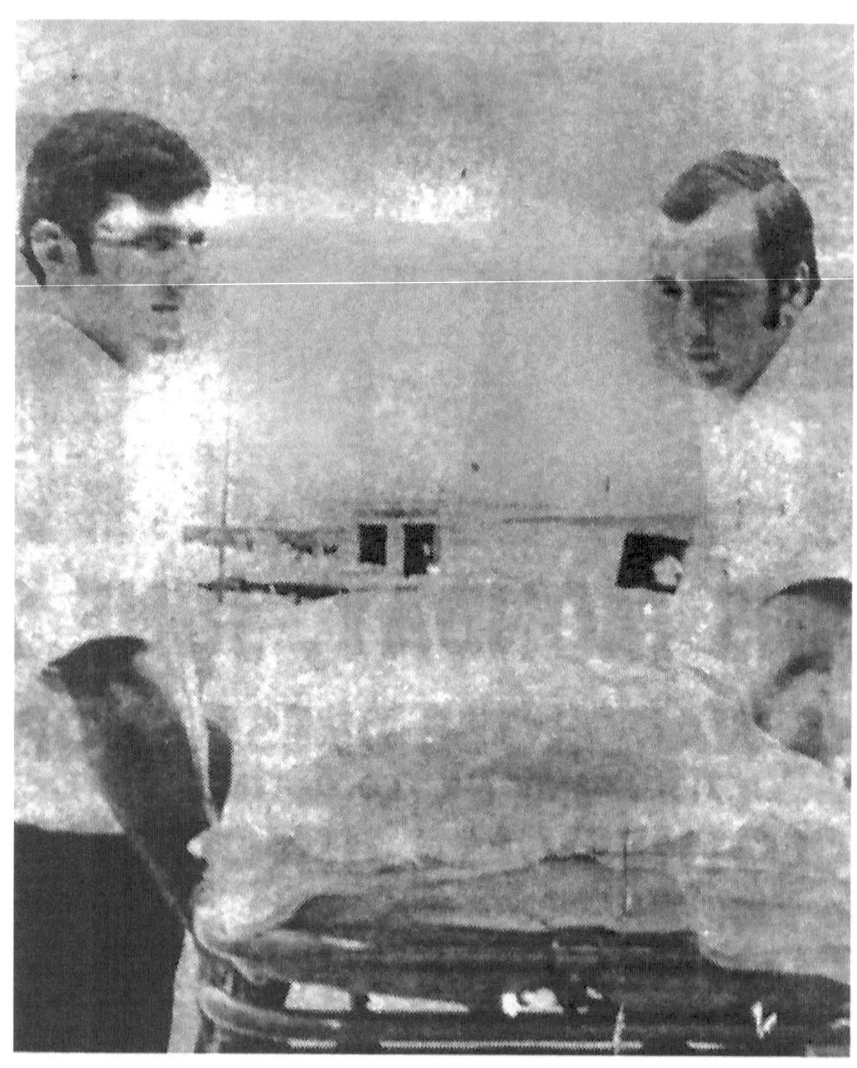

35. Mike LaBelle and Warren Wiley (*Florida Today*, July 12, 1973). The Brevard County Commissioners voted to give Brevard Ambulance Service a contract for $112,000 to serve the North and Central Brevard and HCVAS $70,000 to serve South Brevard ($35,000 for maintenance, gas, oil, and a new ambulance and $35,000 towards a new headquarters).

36. Melbourne Junior Women's Club members Peggy Foster and Mary Halley presenting Edith Koelsch (HCVAS Trustee) with a check for $1200 for the building fund (*Evening Times*, April 19, 1974). Edith was one of the first in the state to complete the Florida Emergency Medical Technician (EMT) course.

July 1, 1974

Federal Communications Commission,
Mr. Charles E. Higginbotham,
Chief, Safety and Special Radio Services Bureau,
Washington, D.C.

Subject: File No. 9099-PS-P/L-18
          Request for Extension of
          Temporary License Authority

Dear Mr. Higginbotham,

We wish to apply for a further extension of our special
temporary authority (period ending 1 August, 1974) for
our ambulance station KJY-809, with the existing terms
of authorization.

Our move to the permanent location is contingent upon
completion of the new building about November, 1974.
In the interim, we request a six months extension of
the attached temporary authority.

                                    Sincerely,

                                    Frank R. Leslie
                                    Communications Officer

FRL/jr

37. Letter written July 1, 1974 to the FCC. Frank Leslie,
    Communications Officer, requested a 6-month extension of
    HCVAS' radio license.

38. Jane Meier standing in front of the first Palm Bay substation. In October 1974, the city donated the old police station and about $1,500 worth of supplies and labor for remodeling. Volunteers who were recruited to help staff the station received classes in rig training and standard and advanced first aid.

39. This ad appeared in the newspaper asking the community for donations towards the new headquarters on Hickory Street. HCVAS hoped to raise $100,000 through mail and door-to-door donations. Zayre Department Store donated a fund-drive headquarters that was set up at the corner of Nasa Boulevard and Babcock Street.

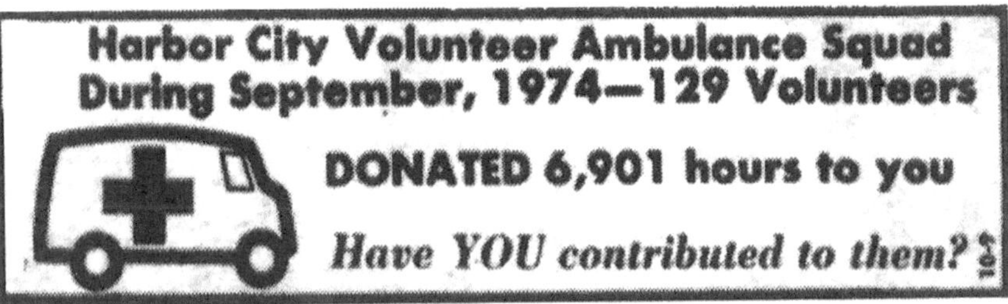

40. This ad placed in the *Evening Times* (October 9, 1974) also asked the community for donations.

41. James Ward from American Legion Post 81 presenting Barbara Cooper and Don Judd (HCVAS president 1974-1976) with a check on December 7, 1974. At this time, HCVAS had 145 volunteers.

II.

Permanent Headquarters and Expansion 1975-1980

42. After almost nine years, HCVAS finally had a permanent headquarters. The City of Melbourne donated the 2.5 acre site at 1131 Hickory Street in Melbourne. Joe DiPrima won the bid to build the 5,266 square foot building at a cost not to exceed $118,000. The concrete block construction, air-conditioning, and underground sprinklers were completed by area contractors at a fraction of their actual cost. Florida Institute of Technology donated palm trees for the landscaping.

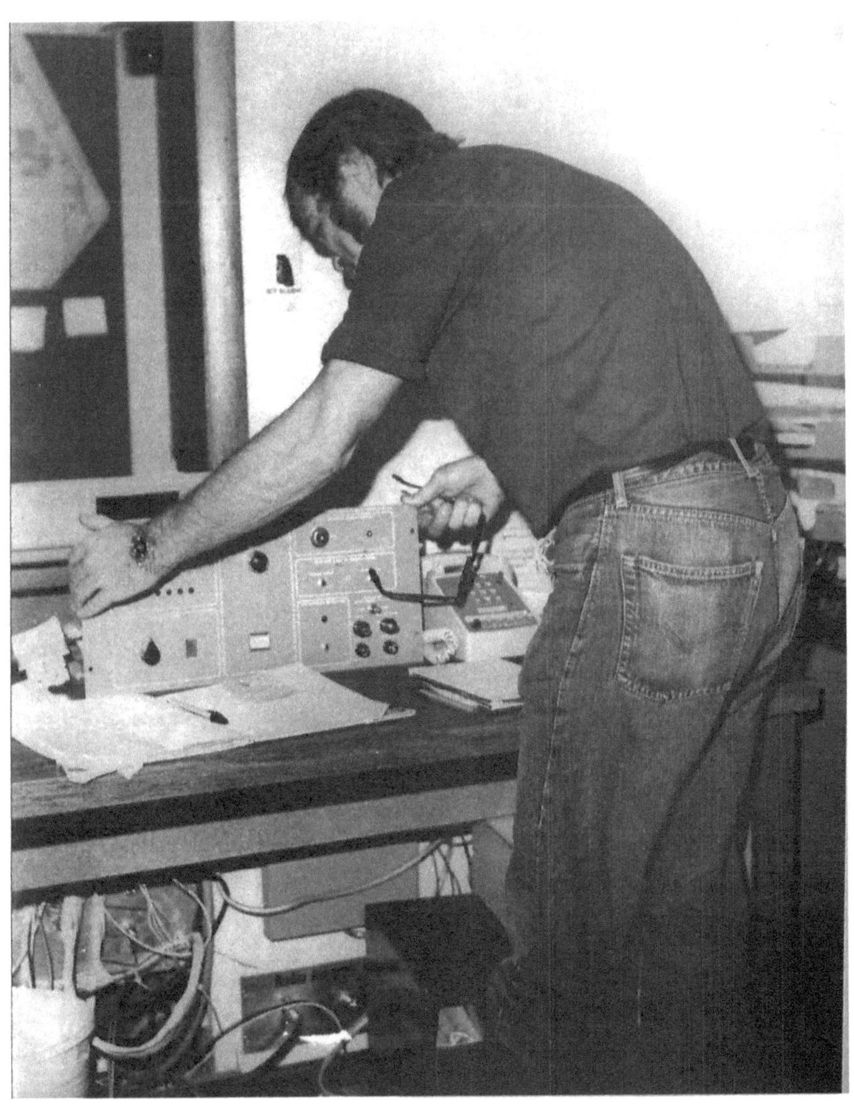

43. A technician setting up the dispatch console at the new headquarters on Hickory Street. HCVAS moved into the new building in November of 1974. Because the squad was a not-for-profit organization, the State Health Department waived the state license fee that would have cost $2,000 annually.

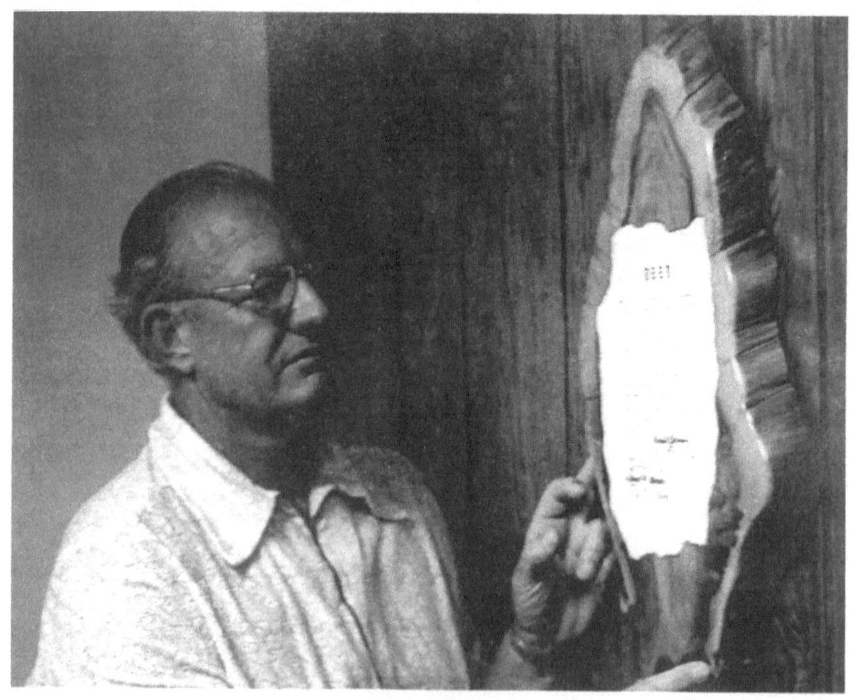

44. Don Judd looking at the deed (mounted in a plaque) to the new headquarters on Hickory Street.

45. A 1975 list of HCVAS board members, officers and members. The squad had 150 active members who served South Brevard with a population of 115,000.

```
                HARBOR CITY VOLUNTEER AMBULANCE SQUAD, INC.

                D E D I C A T I O N     S E R V I C E

                         January 11, 1975


10:30   MUSIC BY THE MELBOURNE MUNICIPAL BAND - A. V. "Chick" Catterton
                                                  Director

11:00   INTRODUCTION OF MASTER OF CEREMONIES   The Honorable Val Steele
                                               County Commissioner Dist.3
          By Board of Governors Member
          The Honorable Dave Barret, State Representative Dist. 44

        INVOCATION - Reverend Frank Cummings
                Former Chaplain, Brevard Hospital

        FLAG RAISING - Melbourne Junior Police League

        NATIONAL ANTHEM - Melbourne Municipal Band

        WELCOME - The Honorable Richard V. Donahue, Mayor of Melbourne

        INTRODUCTION OF GUESTS - The Master of Ceremonies

        DEDICATION ADDRESS - The Honorable Joseph Wickham
                       Brevard County Commissioner, Dist. 5

        REMARKS FROM THE BOARD OF GOVERNORS - Chairman Robert V. Johnson

        RIBBON CUTTING - Mike Sharra, former Board Chairman and
                         Donald Judd, President of Ambulance Squad

        SPECIAL PRESENTATION - Board Chairman Robert V. Johnson

        OPEN HOUSE
```

46. Program for the dedication of the new headquarters. On January
11, 1975, HCVAS dedicated the new building on Hickory Street
as its permanent headquarters.

47. The Melbourne Junior Police League conducting the flag raising ceremony at the January 11, 1975 dedication of the new headquarters on Hickory Street.

48. Dave Barret, State Representative District 44, speaking at
the dedication of the new headquarters on Hickory Street.
Guests included Melbourne Mayor Richard Donahue; County
Commissioners Joe Wickham and Val Steele; Robert V.
Johnson, Chair of the Board of Governors; and Harry Goode.
The Melbourne Municipal Band under the direction of A. V.
Catterton performed during the ceremony.

49. Joseph Wickham, Brevard County Commissioner (District 5), congratulating Don Judd (HCVAS president 1974-6) at the dedication of the new headquarters on Hickory Street.

50. Scott Penrod giving guests at the open house a tour of the ambulance bays while Ricky and Lou Lochlear await their next ambulance call.

51. The South Brevard Homemakers Club provided the refreshments during the two-day open house to celebrate the building dedication.

52. Sandy Diggett demonstrating the dispatch equipment for guests at the open house. The dispatcher's job included receiving and recording calls, alerting crews, pushing a button to lift the bay doors, and using the radio to stay in touch with crews responding to calls.

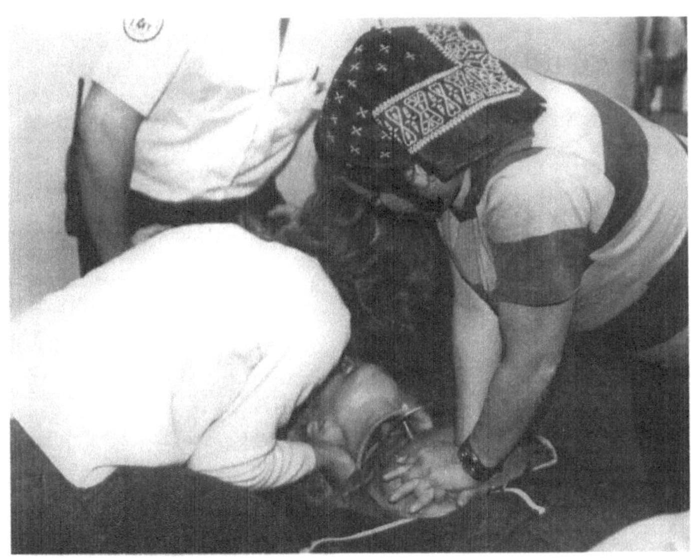

53. Members giving a CPR demonstration for guests at the open house.

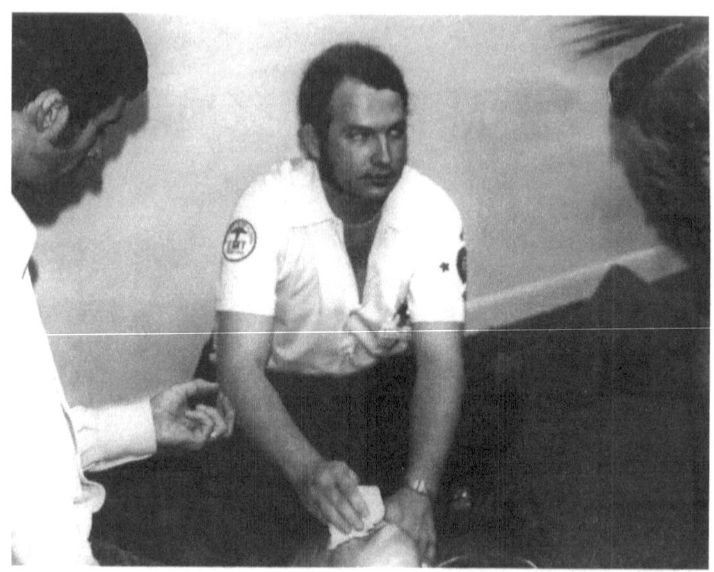

54. Rick Bridges giving a demonstration for guests. Volunteers went through extensive training and a long apprenticeship before riding as ambulance attendants.

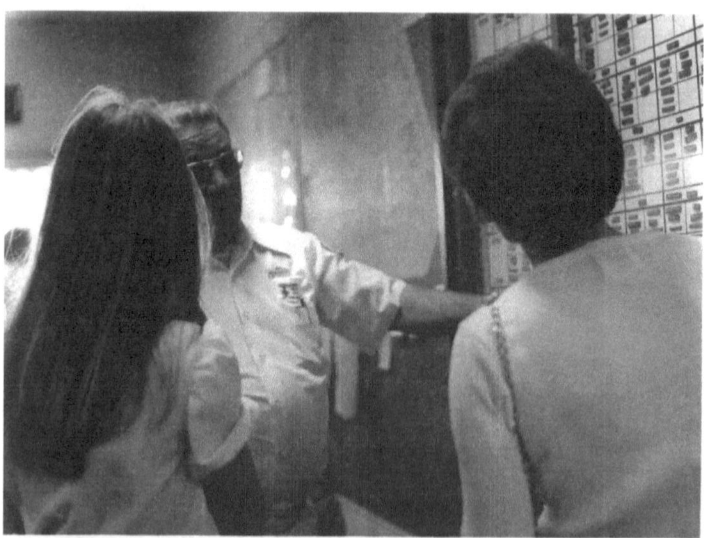

55. Paul Cassidy explaining the crew scheduling board to guests at the open house. Volunteers ranged in age from 16 year-old dispatchers to 70 year-old retirees.

 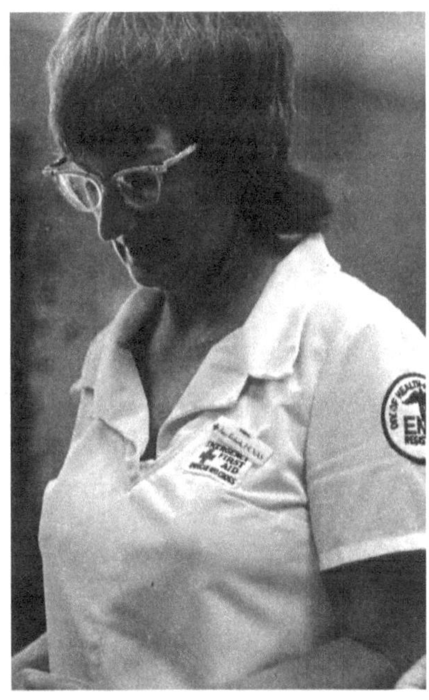

56. Peter Roberts (HCVAS president 1976-8) showing a guest the area maps used by a crew to locate a street when a call came in. HCVAS was now responding to 400 or 500 calls a month.

57. Jean Roberts at the open house. Although privately and publicly subsidized ambulance services charged up to $118.50 to take a family of five three miles to the hospital, HCVAS charged no fee.

58. Al Deluna, a Florida Institute of Technology engineering student, entering the driver's seat to respond to an ambulance call. Volunteers not only included college students but also engineers, teachers, housewives, nurses, and retirees.

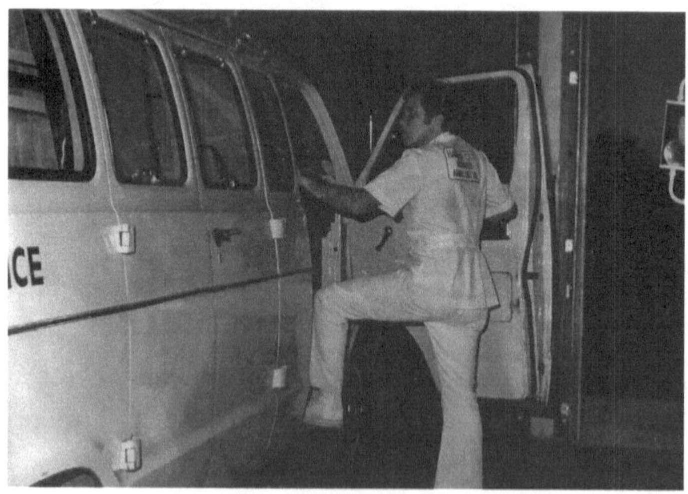

59. Brady Pinkston (another Florida Institute of Technology student) responding to an ambulance call. In 1974, 15 Florida Tech students volunteered at least three hours a week. Fraternities and organizations on campus were encouraged to sponsor fund-raisers and solicit volunteers for HCVAS.

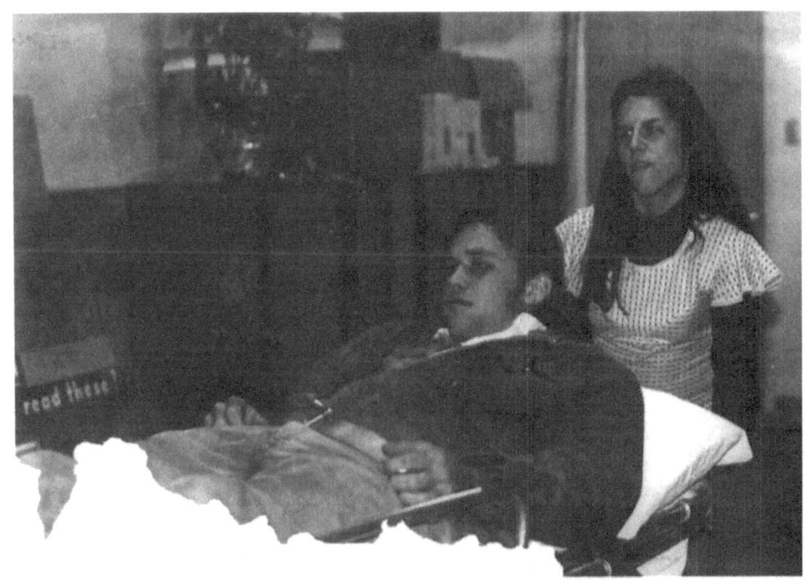

60. John Frey and Debbie Powers demonstrating the stretcher used
on an ambulance.

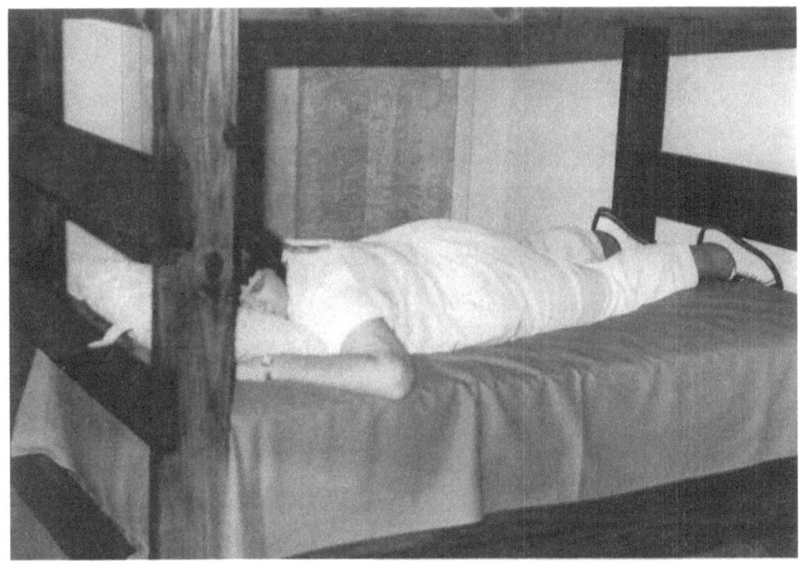

61. Debbie Vaughn catching a quick nap. The headquarters on Hickory
Street had two bunkrooms where crews could rest between calls.
The beds were constructed by Jim Owens and Dick Smolka.

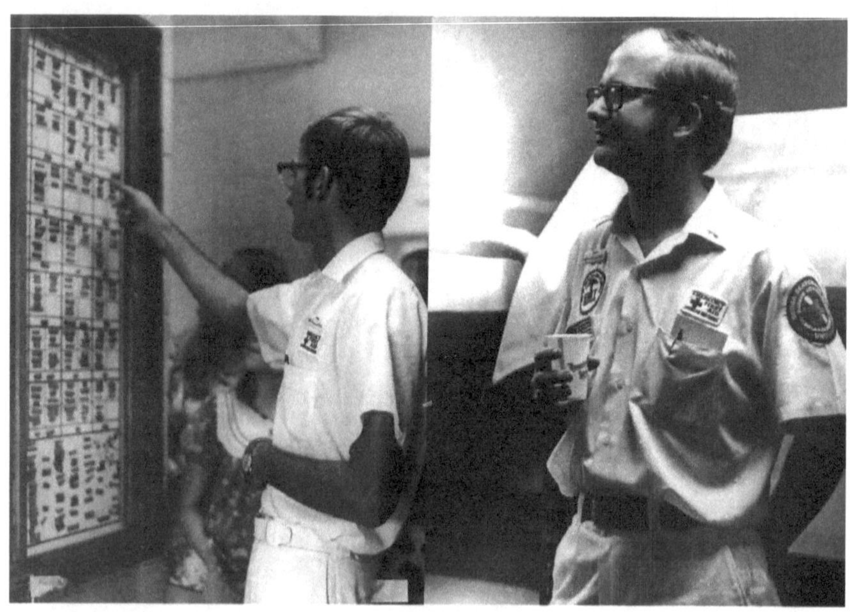

62. Bob Thompson checking his crew assignment on the scheduling board.

63. Frank Leslie wearing a patch on his left shoulder to indicate he was part of the Scuba Search & Rescue Unit (SSRU).

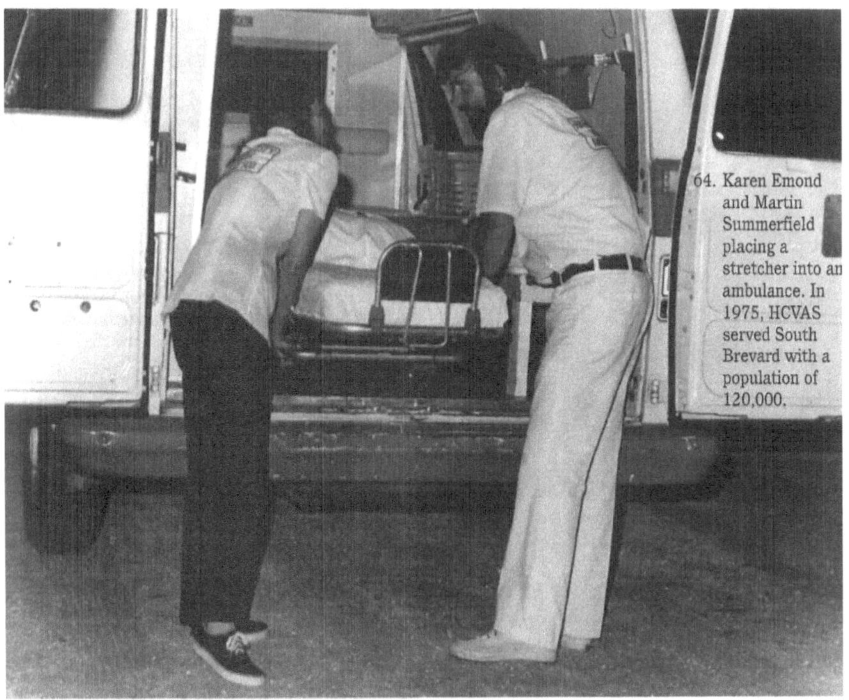

64. Karen Emond and Martin Summerfield placing a stretcher into an ambulance. In 1975, HCVAS served South Brevard with a population of 120,000.

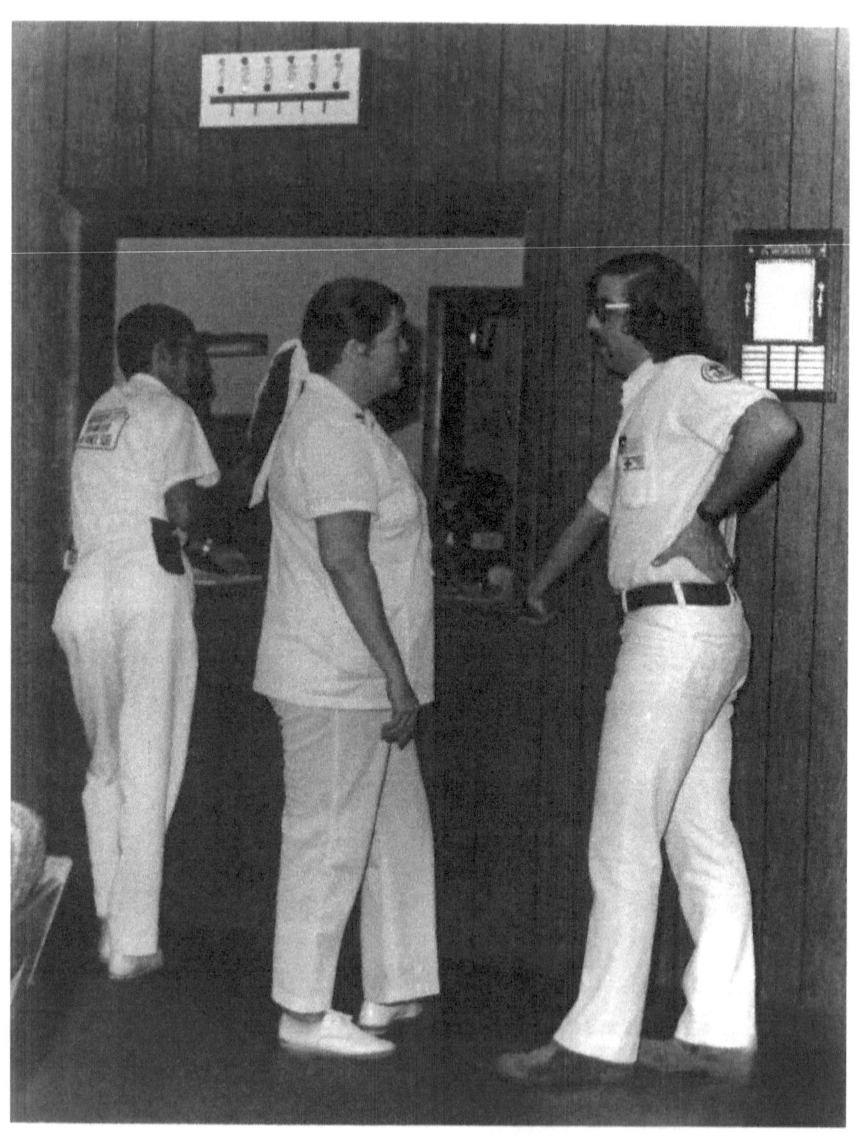

65. Bob Thompson, Peggy Barone, and Al Deluna at a shift change.
Lights above the dispatch window indicated which ambulance
was out on a call.

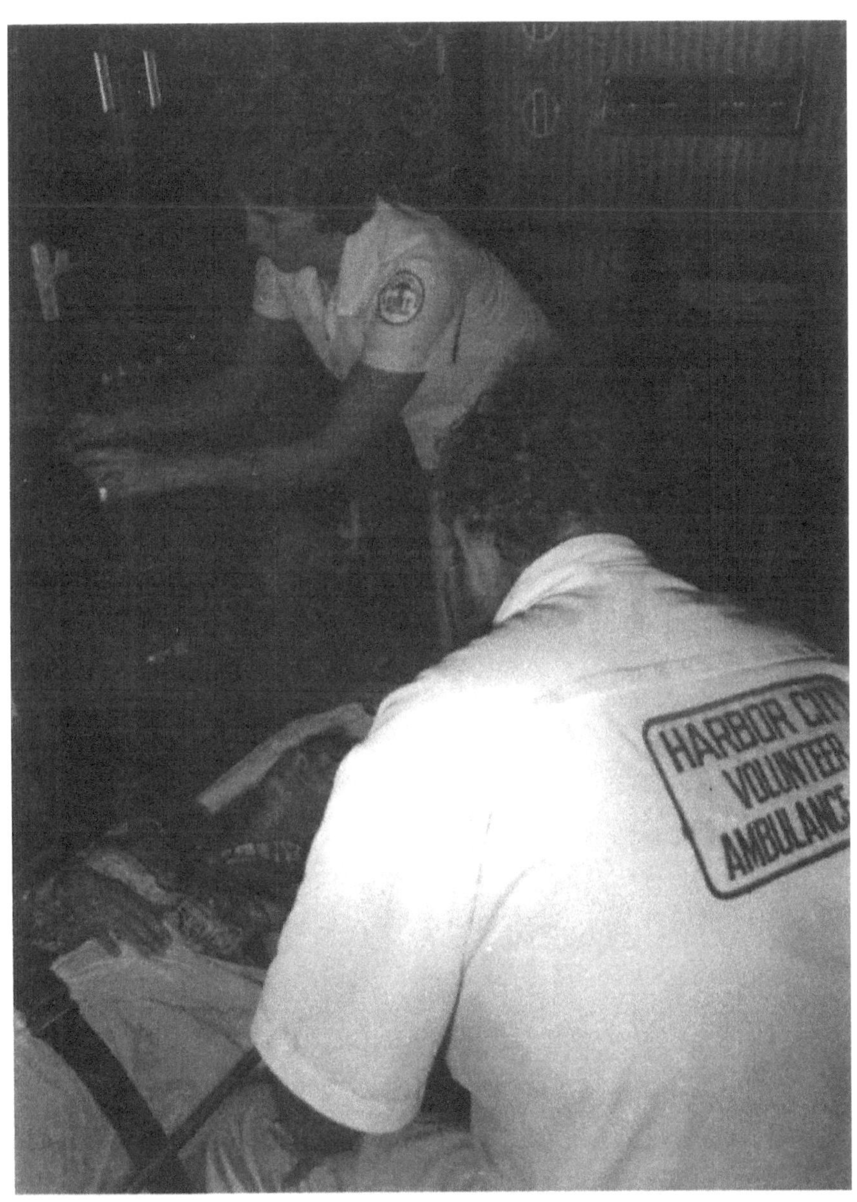

66. Sandy Penrod and Wally Powell attending a patient. In 1975, HCVAS had 180 members, each volunteering on the average 54 hours a month.

67. Heidi Bonn and Sharon Rodier washing Unit 1. Volunteers, in addition to responding to ambulance calls, did maintenance and lawn care at the Hickory Street headquarters.

68. Fleet of 6 units that covered South Brevard out of the Hickory Street headquarters in 1975. An ambulance cost between $15,000 to $16,000 plus another $4,000 to stock the necessary medical supplies and equipment. Each ambulance had to be replaced, on the average, every three years after racking up over 100,000 miles on the road.

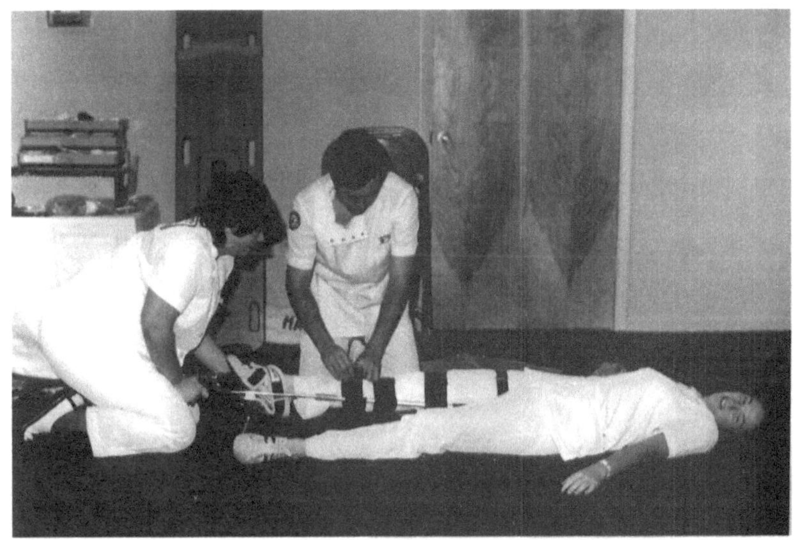

69. Debbie Vaughn, Brady Pawson and Kathy Bibby practice applying the "Hare traction." This standard piece of ambulance equipment was used to immobilize a patient's suspected fractured femur or hip.

70. Louise Owens (HCVAS vice president) giving a report at a 1975 membership meeting in the training room at the Hickory Street headquarters.

71. Janice Cassidy ready to dispatch a call. Dispatchers had to know a list of codes and signals commonly used by fire, police, and Emergency Medical Services.

72. Sandy Penrod, Lester Harrison, Wally Powell, and Linda Ostroff in the "ready room" at headquarters where crews relaxed and waited for emergency calls.

73. Joel Ostroff, a biology professor at Brevard Community College and volunteer EMT, working with Don Judd to reword a proposed bylaw.

74. Elinor Thaxton answering the phone in the dispatch office at the Hickory Street headquarters.

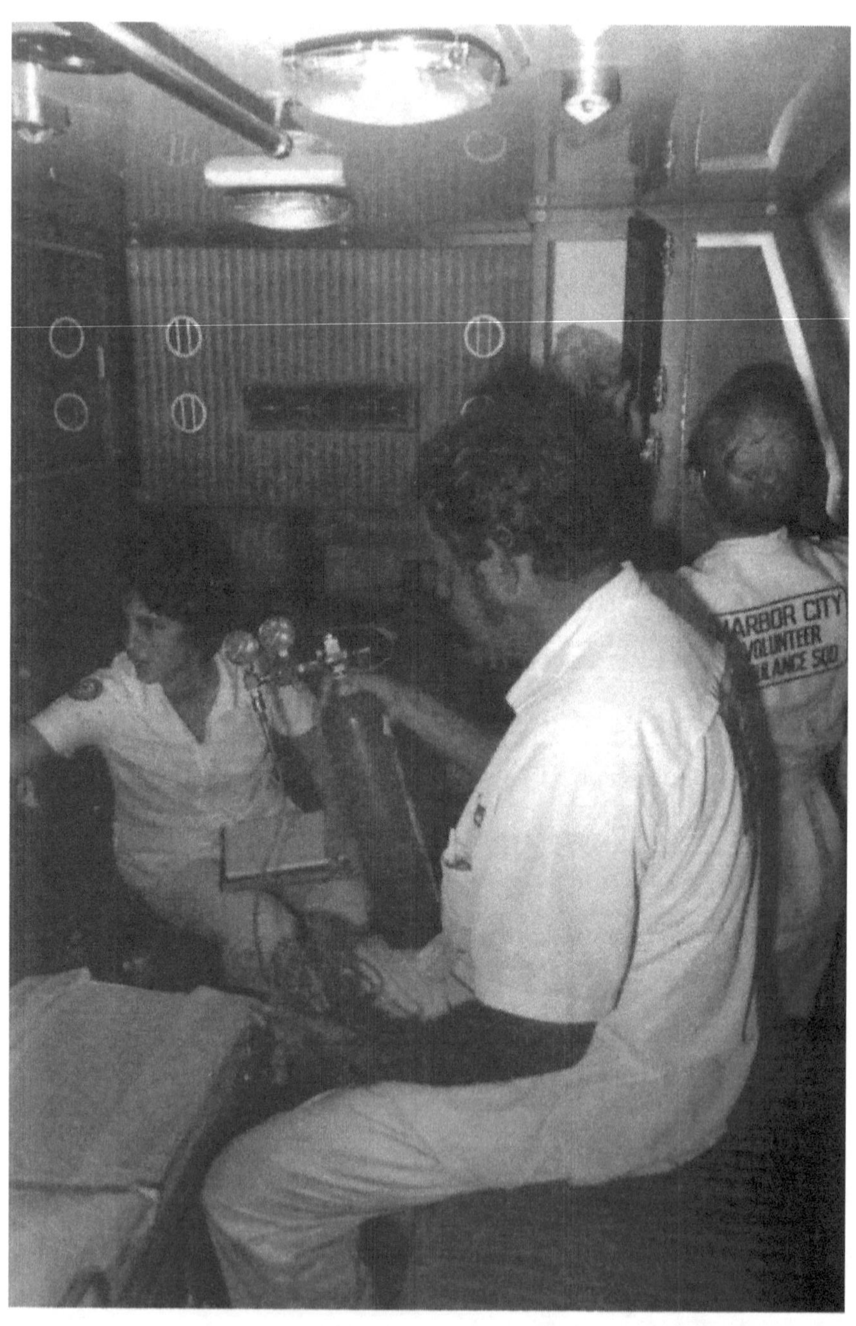

76. Annie Barto doing some administrative work.

77. Karen Emond and Kitty Boone "killing time" between ambulance calls in the "ready room" at the Hickory Street headquarters.

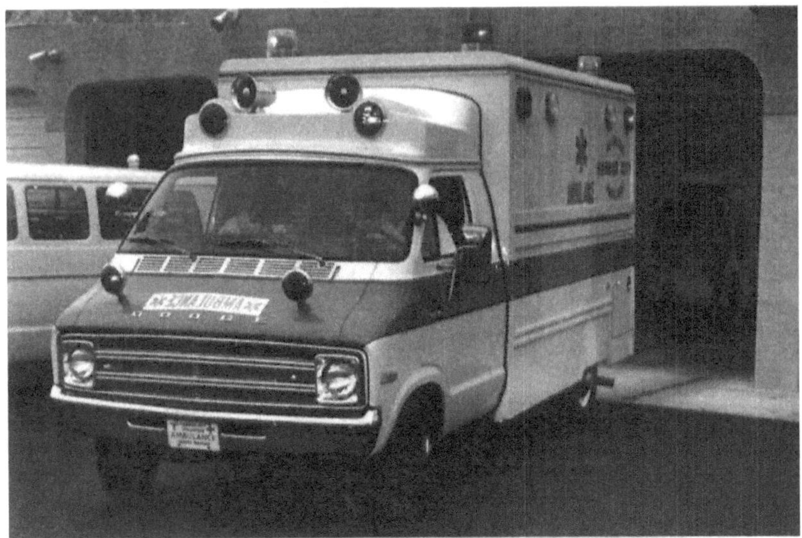

78. Members ready to roll in a new $15,000 modular van (*Florida Today*, May 7, 1975). The van had an advantage over a Cadillac ambulance in that the modular could be shifted to a new truck chassis to extend its "life." A close-up view of the van is shown parked in front of one the bays at the Hickory Street headquarters.

79. Louise Owens and Vicky Deluna attending one of two shooting victims at the Sea Palace restaurant in Melbourne (*Florida Today* 1975).

80. Ben Cowley (left) and Jean Lucas racing toward an emergency call. John Weatherly was the driver (*Florida Today*, September 13, 1976). HCVAS had 6 emergency vehicles and about 200 members who had volunteered 91,000 hours over the past year. Brevard County subsidized the cost of fuel, maintenance and insurance for the ambulances.

THE FLORIDA SENATE
APOLLO BUILDING
333 N. ATLANTIC AVENUE
COCOA BEACH, FLORIDA 32931
305/783-LORI

COMMITTEES:
JUDICIARY-CIVIL
GOVERNMENTAL OPERATIONS
HUMAN RELATIONS COMMISSION
FLORIDA BICENTENNIAL COMMISSION

SENATOR LORI WILSON
16TH DISTRICT

September 16, 1976

The Harbor City Volunteer
  Ambulance Squad, Inc.
1131 S. Hickory Street
Melbourne, FL 32901

Dear Friends:

Congratulations on your 10th Anniversary of service.

Unfortunately, I will be out of town for your open house on September 18th, and my schedule will not permit me to join you then.

Thanks for thinking of me, and my best wishes for another successful 10 years.

independently yours,

Lori Wilson
Senator

DEMPSEY J. BARRON	ALAN TRASK	JOE BROWN	JOHN D. MELTON
President	President Pro Tempore	Secretary	Sergeant at Arms

81. Letter dated September 16, 1976 from Senator Lori Wilson, congratulating HCVAS on its 10th anniversary.

Pilot Club

P.O. Box 1683
Melbourne, Fl 32901
September 16, 1976

Harbor City Volunteer Ambulance Squad, Inc.
1131 S. Hickory Street
Melbourne, Florida 32901

On behalf of the Pilot Club of Melbourne, I wish to extend our sincere
congratulations to each of you on the 10th Anniversary of service for
the Harbor City Volunteer Ambulance Squad.

It is indeed a great pleasure to always hear so many nice comments
about a volunteer group. We hope the next 10 years are even more
successful than the past.

Pilotly,

Jenny P. Gilliam
President

jpg

82. A letter (September 16, 1976) from the Pilot Club in Melbourne
on the occasion of HCVAS' 10th anniversary.

The Harbor City Volunteer

Ambulance Squad, Inc.

1131 S. Hickory Street

cordially invites you to attend
an open house ·
on
September 18th & 19th 11: 00a.m. to 5: 00p.m.

TO HELP US CELEBRATE
OUR 10th ANNIVERSARY

"HELP US HELP YOU"

83. An invitation to an open house on September 18 and 19, 1976,
celebrating HCVAS' 10th anniversary.

84. Vance Harless with a cake and guests attending the open house to celebrate HCVAS' 10th anniversary. The squad's 200 members each volunteered at least 12 hours a month.

85. Flyer soliciting volunteers. Although most commercial ambulance services carried two-member crews, HCVAS operated with three-member crews.

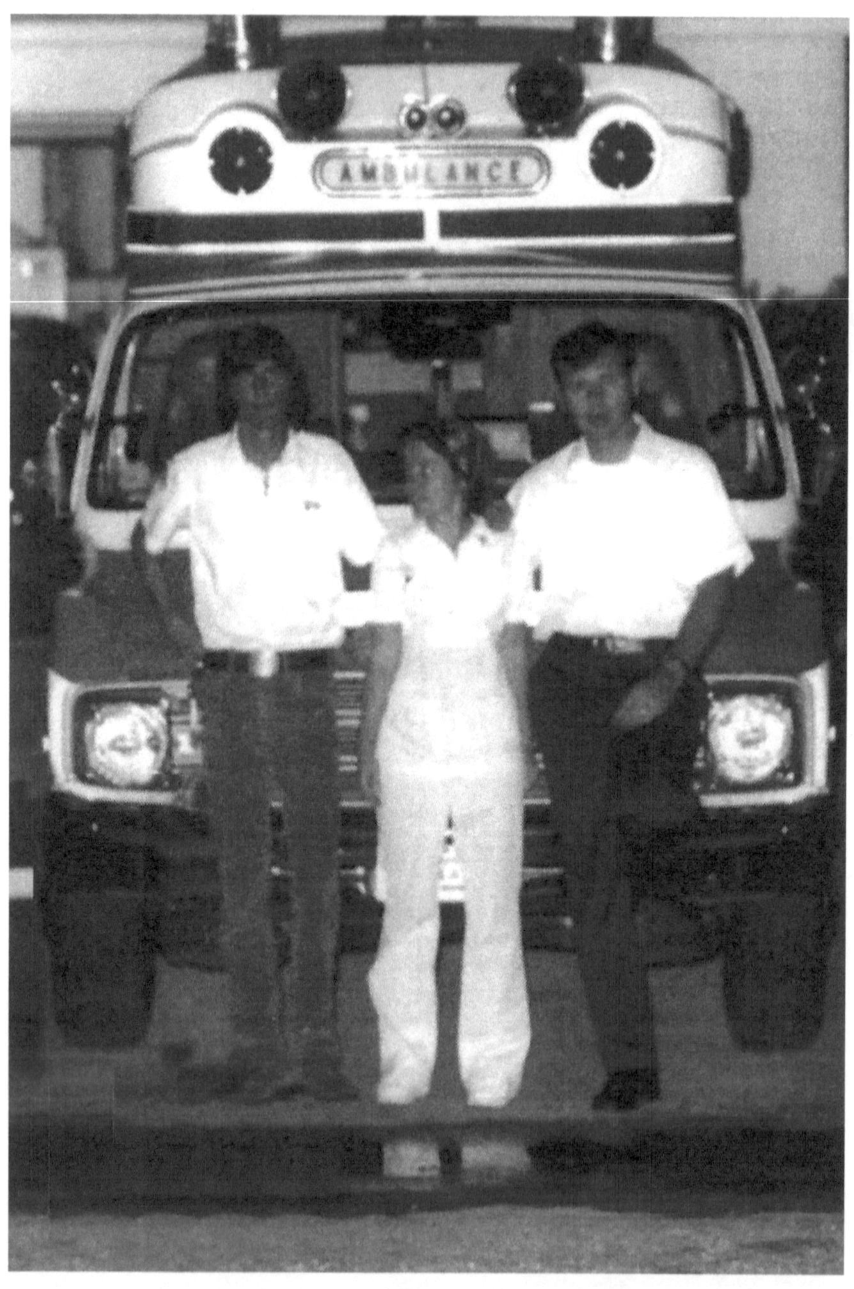

86. Mike Hunt, Nikki Smith, and Scott Penrod standing in front of Unit 1 (1977).

87. Pam Coker, Steve Ellis, Steve Raye, and Janice Cassidy (1976). By now more than half the volunteers were registered EMTs, having taken the 80-hour course.

88. Unit 1 responding to a call (1977).

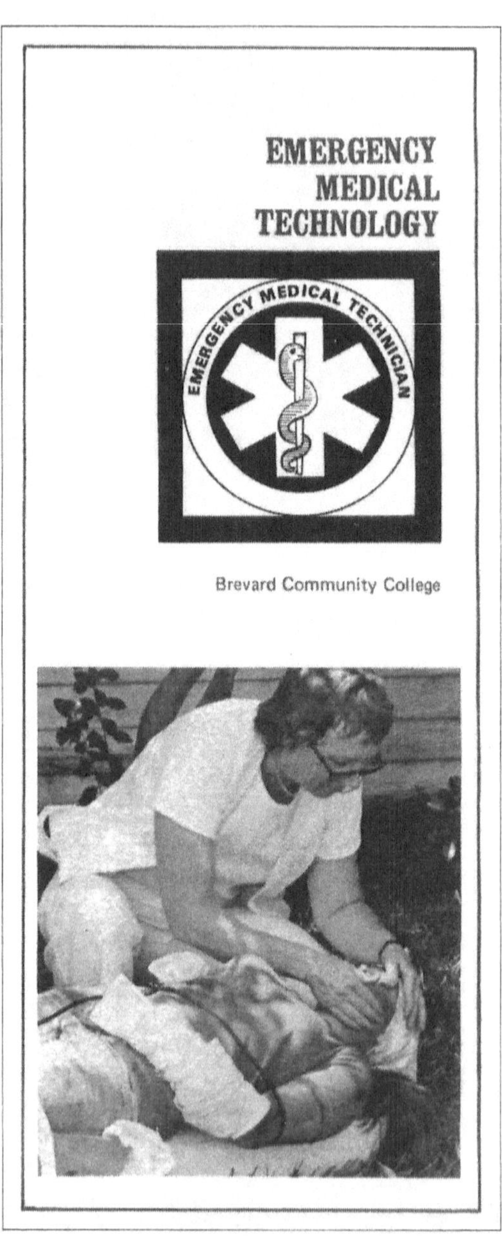

89. A brochure advertising the EMT II class (paramedic level) at Brevard Community College (1977). Featured on the brochure is Louise Owens, who was one of the first members to take the course.

90. Roger Templar, wounded in January 1971 while serving as a Green Beret in Vietnam, volunteered as a HCVAS dispatcher (*Florida Today*, 1978).

91. A 1978 ad listing HCVAS' many services. Now 17 members were paramedics, trained to give advanced life support. They could dispense drugs, start intravenous solutions and give electrical shocks to cardiac victims. The squad had acquired radio equipment and portable electrocardiograms but needed $25,000 for special monitoring and communications equipment and $7,000 for a base station receiver. The squad also needed a community physician to take on the responsibility of serving as its medical director.

```
                                            Troop 300
                                            St. Paul's United
                                            Methodist Church


     The Harbor City Volunteer Ambulance Squad
     1131 S. Hickory St.
     Melbourne, Fla.  32901

     Dear Squad Members,

          On Friday night, May 14th in the Boy Scout Area of Wickham
     Park, a young scout received a neck injury.  The response on the
     part of H.C.A.S. was quick; the crew was outstanding in the way
     they checked, prepared and transported the scout.
          The knowledge of their job, the care and concern they felt
     was visible for all to see.  They were a credit to the Squad and
     to themselves.  THEY WERE JUST GREAT!
          The Scoutmaster, Mr. Fred Peterson, and I, the camp leader,
     wish to thank the following people: the driver, Tom Williams,
     Rick Bridges, and Vicki Zennis.  We would also like to extend
     our graditude to Mr. Ted Burghardt, EMT, for his on-the-spot
     aide and care of this young man.
          There are not enough words to express our thanks for
     these outstanding people.  Troop 300 salutes them.



                                   Thank you very much,

                                   Burke Berckhemer
                                   Burke Berckhemer
                                   Asst. Scoutmaster
                                   Troop 300
```

92. A letter (1979) from Burke Berckhemer, Asst. Scoutmaster of
Troop 300, thanking the crew (Tom Williams, Rick Bridges,
and Vicki Zennis) for treating an injured scout. Ted Burghardt,
HCVAS EMT, was also thanked for rendering immediate care
to the scout.

93. Jane Meier shown with Lori Ellison and Vicki Marsden taking breaks between ambulance calls. With the increase in South Brevard's population, HCVAS needed more volunteers. The dropout rate of members was a constant headache for the squad. "Alternatives included having existing volunteers pull longer shifts, switching some to paid positions or disbanding the squad," said Bob Johnson, President of HCVAS Board of Directors.

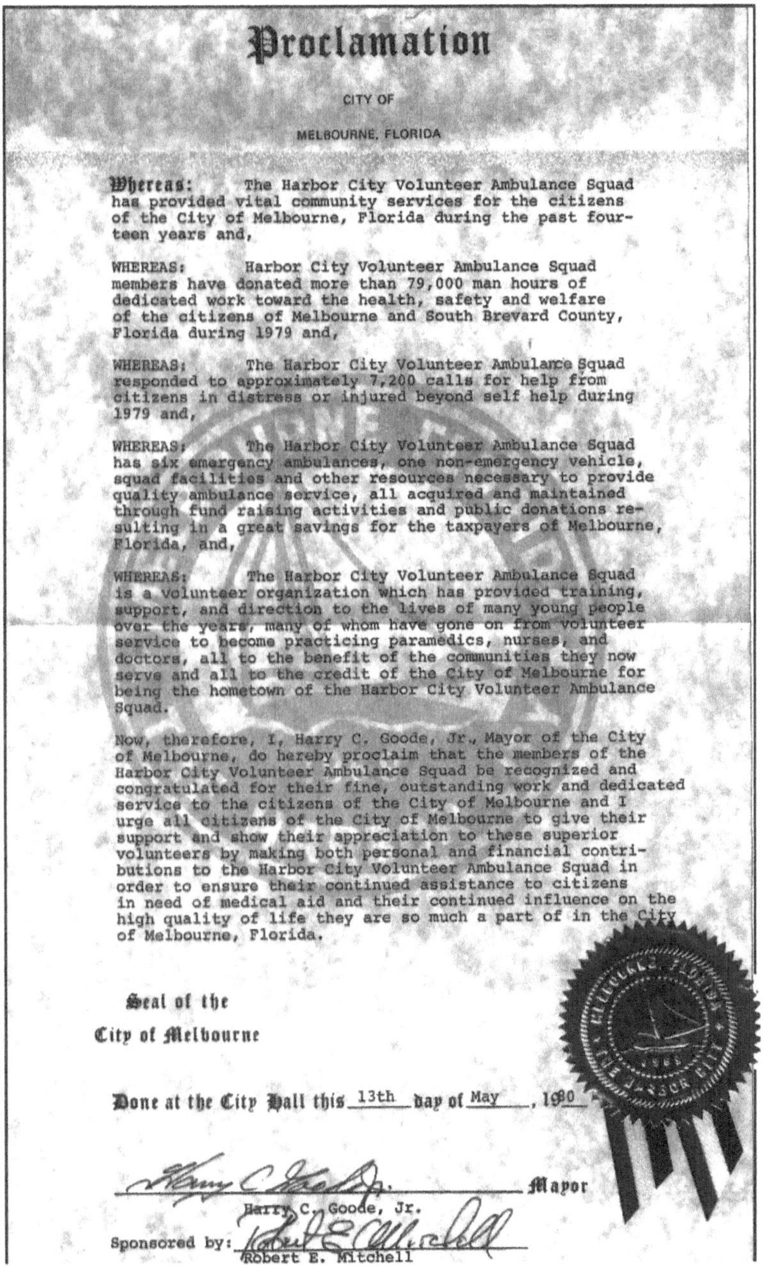

Proclamation

CITY OF

MELBOURNE, FLORIDA

Whereas: The Harbor City Volunteer Ambulance Squad has provided vital community services for the citizens of the City of Melbourne, Florida during the past fourteen years and,

WHEREAS: Harbor City Volunteer Ambulance Squad members have donated more than 79,000 man hours of dedicated work toward the health, safety and welfare of the citizens of Melbourne and South Brevard County, Florida during 1979 and,

WHEREAS: The Harbor City Volunteer Ambulance Squad responded to approximately 7,200 calls for help from citizens in distress or injured beyond self help during 1979 and,

WHEREAS: The Harbor City Volunteer Ambulance Squad has six emergency ambulances, one non-emergency vehicle, squad facilities and other resources necessary to provide quality ambulance service, all acquired and maintained through fund raising activities and public donations resulting in a great savings for the taxpayers of Melbourne, Florida, and,

WHEREAS: The Harbor City Volunteer Ambulance Squad is a volunteer organization which has provided training, support, and direction to the lives of many young people over the years, many of whom have gone on from volunteer service to become practicing paramedics, nurses, and doctors, all to the benefit of the communities they now serve and all to the credit of the City of Melbourne for being the hometown of the Harbor City Volunteer Ambulance Squad.

Now, therefore, I, Harry C. Goode, Jr., Mayor of the City of Melbourne, do hereby proclaim that the members of the Harbor City Volunteer Ambulance Squad be recognized and congratulated for their fine, outstanding work and dedicated service to the citizens of the City of Melbourne and I urge all citizens of the City of Melbourne to give their support and show their appreciation to these superior volunteers by making both personal and financial contributions to the Harbor City Volunteer Ambulance Squad in order to ensure their continued assistance to citizens in need of medical aid and their continued influence on the high quality of life they are so much a part of in the City of Melbourne, Florida.

Seal of the

City of Melbourne

Done at the City Hall this __13th__ day of __May__, 1980

_______________________________ Mayor
Harry C. Goode, Jr.

Sponsored by: _______________________________
Robert E. Mitchell

94. Proclamation given by the City of Melbourne on May 13, 1980 and signed by Mayor Harry Goode, Jr. It acknowledged HCVAS' 14 years of service to the community.

95. Ads asking the community for donations during HCVAS' 1980 fund drive (October 12-18). Money was needed to replace aging ambulances and buy new equipment.

HARBOR CITY VOLUNTEER AMBULANCE SQUAD
1980 FUND DRIVE OCTOBER 12th to 18th

PROVIDING FREE EMERGENCY MEDICAL SERVICE TO THE RESIDENTS OF SOUTH BREVARD SINCE 1966. PLUS ESSENTIAL SHORT AND LONG DISTANCE TRANSPORT SERVICES THROUGHOUT FLORIDA FOR THE BEDRIDDEN, FREE LOAN OF WHEELCHAIRS AND CRUTCHES TO THE NEEDY AND FIRST AID AND CPR CLASSES TO NATIONAL STANDARDS FOR THE GENERAL PUBLIC.

THIS EFFORT IS PROVIDED BY UNPAID VOLUNTEERS DONATING WELL IN EXCESS OF 70,000 HOURS EACH YEAR. RESPONDING TO OVER 600 EMERGENCY CALLS EACH MONTH OVER AN AREA OF 344 SQ. MILES.

DURING THE COMING YEAR IT IS PLANNED TO INTRODUCE ADVANCED LIFE SUPPORT SERVICES TO SOUTH BREVARD COUNTY. A SMALL NUMBER OF PAID PARAMEDICS WILL BE NEEDED TO SUPPLEMENT THE EXISTING VOLUNTEERS AND A FULL TIME PAID OFFICE MANAGER IS NOW NECESSARY TO HANDLE THE ADMINISTRATIVE WORKLOAD. THIS WILL BE DONE WITHOUT PREJUDICE TO THE VOLUNTEERS PLEDGE TO CONTINUE THIS MOST VITAL SERVICE AT NO COST TO THE PATIENT.

BUT — THE FINANCIAL FACTS OF LIFE ARE:

1. IT COSTS APPROX. 20 DOLLARS EACH TIME AN AMBULANCE RESPONDS TO A CALL.

2. FLORIDA STATE REGULATIONS REQUIRE AN AMBULANCE TO BE REPLACED EVERY 3 YRS. THAT'S TWO NEW VEHICLES EACH YEAR AT A COST APPROACHING 25,000 DOLLARS EACH.

3. MEDICAL SUPPLIES, EQUIPMENT, OXYGEN AND THE MAINTENANCE OF A HEADQUARTERS AND TWO SATELLITE STATIONS BRINGS ANNUAL OPERATING COSTS TO NEARLY 150,000 DOLLARS.

4. ADVANCED LIFE SUPPORT SERVICE, THE ENORMOUS INCREASE IN ADMINISTRATIVE DEMANDS REQUIRING A SMALL NUMBER OF PAID MEMBERS AND THE TRAINING OF MORE UNPAID VOLUNTEERS TO SUPPORT THESE NEEDS WILL ADD TO THE FINANCIAL REQUIREMENTS.

5. THE COST OF PROPER UNIFORMS IS BECOMING BEYOND THE REACH OF MANY OF THE YOUNGER VOLUNTEERS AND A UNIFORM PURCHASE PROGRAM MUST BE CONSIDERED.

6. WHILE REQUESTS FOR ADDITIONAL COUNTY SUBSIDY HAS BEEN MADE, THIS WILL BE FAR BELOW THAT NECESSARY TO FUNCTION WITHOUT INCREASED PUBLIC SUPPORT.

THE OVERALL COST TO OPERATE, HOWEVER, WILL BE LITTLE MORE THAN ONE QUARTER OF THAT FOR A COUNTY PROVIDED SYSTEM WHICH IN THESE INFLATIONARY TIMES CANNOT BE IGNORED BY ANY TAXPAYER.

RESIDENTS OF SOUTH BREVARD COUNTY
THE VOLUNTEERS NEED YOUR
FINANCIAL ASSISTANCE

PLEASE SEND YOUR TAX DEDUCTIBLE DONATION TO: THE FUND DRIVE DIRECTOR, HARBOR CITY VOLUNTEER AMBULANCE SQUAD, 1131 S. HICKORY STREET MELBOURNE 32901 724-4411

Donations received thru 31 Dec. 1980 will be included in this fund drive.

96. Members at a party given by Jane Meier in 1980.

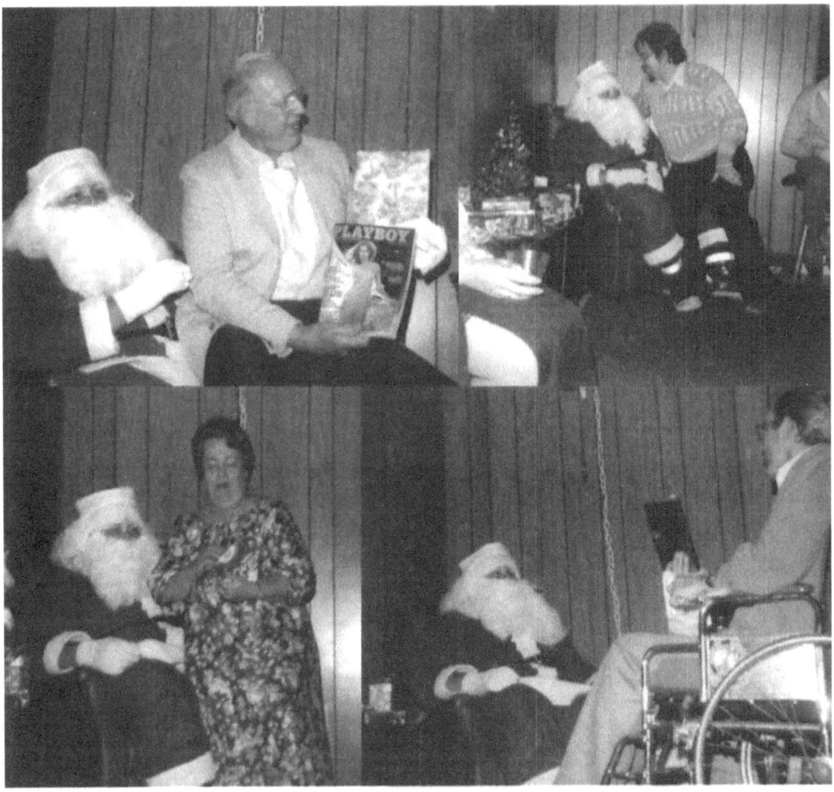

97. Members at a Christmas party given by Margaret and John Weatherly (HCVAS president 1981-2) in 1980. Doug Van Meter played Santa Claus.

III.

From BLS to ALS 1981-1986

98. Harris employees who were HCVAS volunteers: Frank Leslie, Jim Irvin (driver), Debbie Vaughn, John Weatherly, Eunice Willingham, Robert Thompson, Mike Malley and Bill Whitehead (Harris Corporation newsletter 1981).

99. Jim Irvin and Judy Carter, volunteer EMTs, waiting for an ambulance call in the "ready room" at the Hickory Street headquarters. Jim was a senior engineer at Harris Corp., and Judy worked for the Graduate Admissions Office at Florida Institute of Technology. HCVAS had about 200 volunteers and now responded to 600 or 700 calls a month (1981).

100. Sharon Irvin, an Assistant Professor of English at Florida Institute of Technology, dispatching at the Hickory Street headquarters (1981). Behind her is the console that the dispatchers used to indicate which ambulance was on a call, which one was up next in the rotation, and which one was down for maintenance.

101. Don Willingham and Jane Meier in front of the Hickory Street headquarters. Jane served as HCVAS vice president (1979-80) and Public Relations Director (1981). Don joined HCVAS as part of the first group of 40 volunteers and served as trustee, vice-president, and president (1971-74).

102. An ad placed in the newspaper asking for volunteers. In 1981, HCVAS had 180 members, but not all were "riding" members. Some were dispatchers and office workers.

103. Damage from the March 27, 1981 collapse of Harbour Cay condominium in Cocoa Beach, where 11 workers were killed and 23 injured (*Florida Today*, March 28, 1981). HCVAS sent its beach unit and back-up unit from the Hickory Street headquarters to assist the county crews. They worked in ankle-deep liquid concrete to tend the injured and dying and then made four runs to Cape Canaveral Hospital.

Contact: Jane Meier
724-4411

EMERGENCY TELEPHONE:
BUSINESS TELEPHONE:

FOR IMMEDIATE RELEASE (3/30/81)
VOLUNTEERS DISASTER PLAN PUT TO TEST

Harbor City Volunteer Ambulance Squad's disaster plan was put to the test last Friday, March 27, when the Harbor Cay condominium collapsed in Cocoa Beach

As soon as County ambulance dispatchers were notified of the disaster, Charlie Gilboard immediately sent his beach unit and a back up unit from the Melbourne headquarters to the disaster scene. A dispatcher under training, Keith Ball, commenced calling in key personnel and extra crews from their homes and work places

Within a few minutes the group's Squad Commander, Jeff Bass and two assistant squad commanders along with enough crew members to staff all available ambulances were at the station and ready to respond

These units were held in reserve at the request of Civil Defense headquarters in Rockledge but they were not idle. One unit was sent to the beach and others backed up the main base crew for accident and illness calls in the Melbourne area.

Crews who had been sent to the disaster site worked ankle deep in liquid concrete to tend the injured and dying. They made four runs to Cape Canaveral Hospital with patients

Later came the task of cleaning up themselves and their equipment. One volunteer had to pour a liter of saline solution normally used on burns, into his shoe to release his foot from the setting cement. Ambulances had to be scrubbed to remove concrete residue which had covered the patients and the legs of the crew members

The Squad's President, John Weatherley, said that he had the greatest confidence in the members' capability to respond to this kind of problem. It's one of the advantages of a volunteer organization, because you need more people to run a routine operation, you have more in reserve when this sort of thing happens.

If this had happened in South Brevard we could have had at least fifty Emergency Medical Technicians on the scene in an hour or so along with every available ambulance We know that our colleagues in the County EMS would also provide assistance if needed just as we were able to do for them.

104. Copy of HCVAS press release dated March 30, 1981 about the Harbour Cay disaster. The incident put the squad's disaster plan to the test.

105. Pamela (PJ) Cawley, one of the three paramedics hired in 1981 (the other two were John Barone and Tony Mincu). Dr. Steve Miley, the Medical Director of HRMC (Holmes Regional Medical Center) Emergency Department, agreed to become HCVAS' second medical director. On May 1, two of the squad's ambulances were equipped for advanced life-support (ALS). Two ambulances would be dispatched to a scene, with the BLS (basic life support) unit staffed with an EMT responding first. The ALS unit followed but was sent back to headquarters if a paramedic was not needed.

106. Judy Cavasos, a nurse at HRMC and HCVAS volunteer, conducting a class in reading EKG strips at the Hickory Street headquarters. Members now were required to undergo more training in order to give advanced medical care to patients.

107. Members celebrating HCVAS' 15th anniversary in 1981. At this time, the squad standardized the uniforms members wore: white shirt with black pants, belt, sox and shoes.

108. Tom Uzel and Karrie Terranova receiving a $1,000 donation
     from Keith Storm of the Port Malabar County Club Pro AM
     Golf Tour (*Palm Bay News*, August 17, 1984). Karrie became
     HCVAS' first fulltime administrative supervisor (1982).
     HRMCs executive committee at first wanted to stop HCVAS
     from providing advanced medical care and turn all critical care
     patients over to the county. They agreed to work with HCVAS
     if it restructured its board and hired more paramedics and a
     full-time administrator. In February 1982, the squad was put
     on a 90-day trial period to see if its new ALS system was
     working efficiently. At the end of the trial period, the medical
     community was satisfied with the quality of HCVAS' medical
     care.

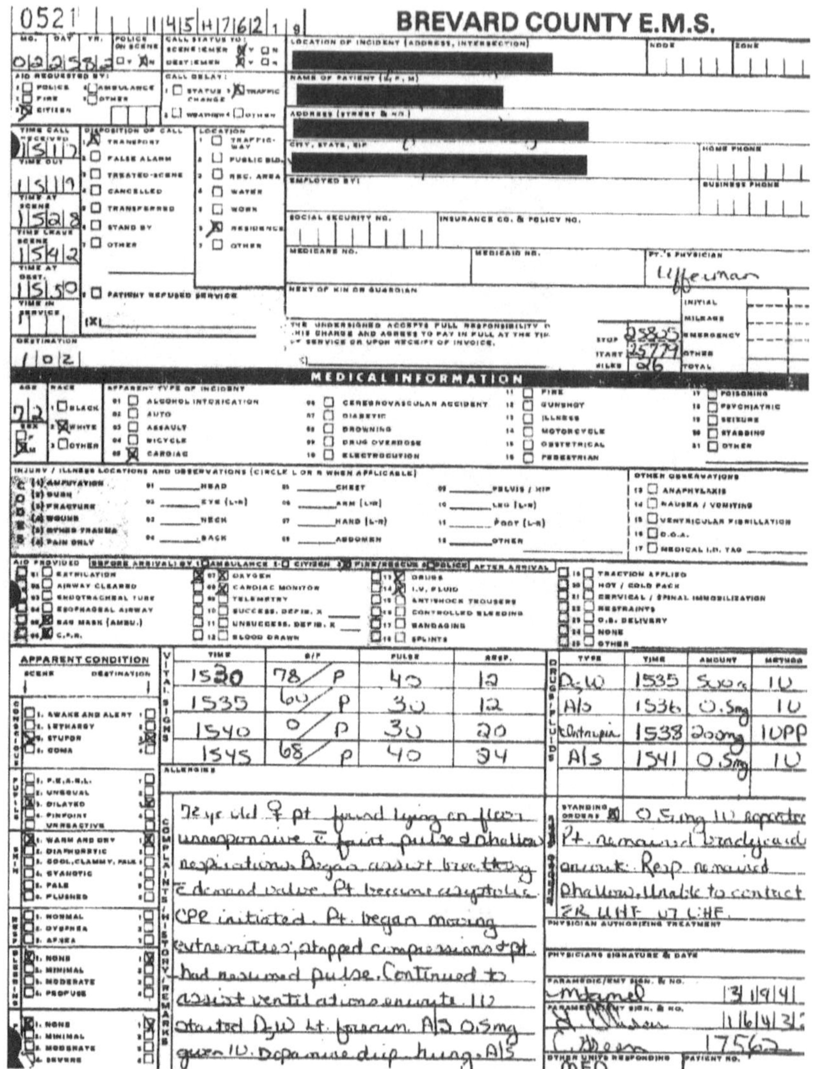

109. An early ALS call dated February 25, 1982 (crew: Max Hammel, Lori Ellison, and C. Green). The cost of moving to ALS doubled the squad's budget from $150,000 to $245,000. The squad as yet did not charge for its services, although the same service from a private ambulance would have cost a patient between $90.00 to $200.00 per run. About 85% of the HCVAS' operating costs came from donations and the rest from a county subsidy.

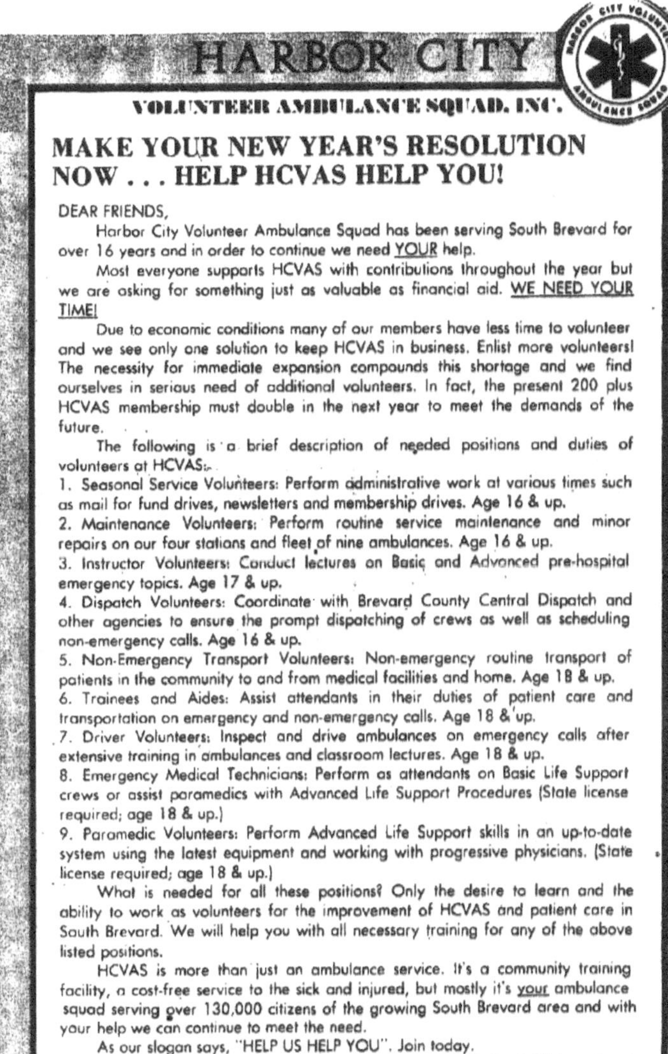

HARBOR CITY
VOLUNTEER AMBULANCE SQUAD, INC.

MAKE YOUR NEW YEAR'S RESOLUTION NOW . . . HELP HCVAS HELP YOU!

DEAR FRIENDS,

Harbor City Volunteer Ambulance Squad has been serving South Brevard for over 16 years and in order to continue we need YOUR help.

Most everyone supports HCVAS with contributions throughout the year but we are asking for something just as valuable as financial aid. WE NEED YOUR TIME!

Due to economic conditions many of our members have less time to volunteer and we see only one solution to keep HCVAS in business. Enlist more volunteers! The necessity for immediate expansion compounds this shortage and we find ourselves in serious need of additional volunteers. In fact, the present 200 plus HCVAS membership must double in the next year to meet the demands of the future.

The following is a brief description of needed positions and duties of volunteers at HCVAS:

1. Seasonal Service Volunteers: Perform administrative work at various times such as mail for fund drives, newsletters and membership drives. Age 16 & up.

2. Maintenance Volunteers: Perform routine service maintenance and minor repairs on our four stations and fleet of nine ambulances. Age 16 & up.

3. Instructor Volunteers: Conduct lectures on Basic and Advanced pre-hospital emergency topics. Age 17 & up.

4. Dispatch Volunteers: Coordinate with Brevard County Central Dispatch and other agencies to ensure the prompt dispatching of crews as well as scheduling non-emergency calls. Age 16 & up.

5. Non-Emergency Transport Volunteers: Non-emergency routine transport of patients in the community to and from medical facilities and home. Age 18 & up.

6. Trainees and Aides: Assist attendants in their duties of patient care and transportation on emergency and non-emergency calls. Age 18 & up.

7. Driver Volunteers: Inspect and drive ambulances on emergency calls after extensive training in ambulances and classroom lectures. Age 18 & up.

8. Emergency Medical Technicians: Perform as attendants on Basic Life Support crews or assist paramedics with Advanced Life Support Procedures (State license required; age 18 & up.)

9. Paramedic Volunteers: Perform Advanced Life Support skills in an up-to-date system using the latest equipment and working with progressive physicians. (State license required; age 18 & up.)

What is needed for all these positions? Only the desire to learn and the ability to work as volunteers for the improvement of HCVAS and patient care in South Brevard. We will help you with all necessary training for any of the above listed positions.

HCVAS is more than just an ambulance service. It's a community training facility, a cost-free service to the sick and injured, but mostly it's your ambulance squad serving over 130,000 citizens of the growing South Brevard area and with your help we can continue to meet the need.

As our slogan says, "HELP US HELP YOU". Join today.

For further information stop by our main base at 1131 South Hickory Street just north of Holmes Regional Medical Center.

Thank you,

DENNIS TYLER
PRESIDENT

110. An ad placed in the newspaper asking for volunteers. HCVAS had about 200 members but wanted to double membership to meet future demands.

111. Members and guests at an HCVAS picnic at Wickham Park
in 1982.

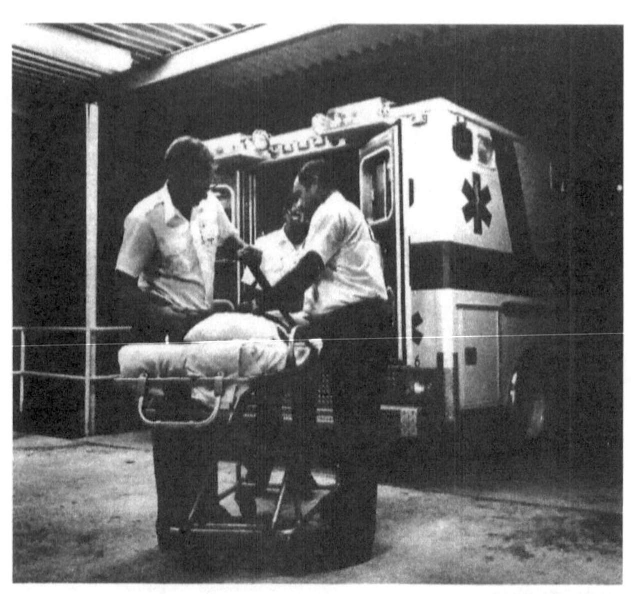

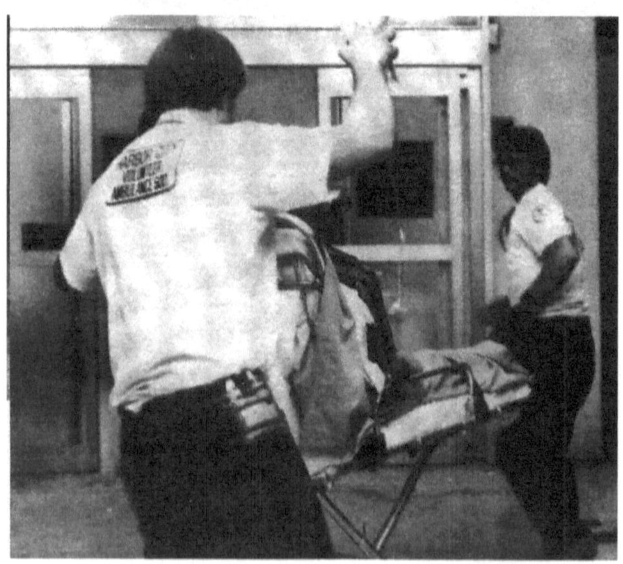

112. HCVAS members featured in *Focus* (*Holmes Regional Medical Center, Vol 2, Number 1*: Winter 1983). The journal examined emergency medical services and the role of the paramedic. In 1983, HCVAS had 9 paid and 6 volunteer paramedics, one riding on each crew. Some of the paramedics shown are Bill Scholl, Laddie Rutkowski, and intern Vicki Marsden.

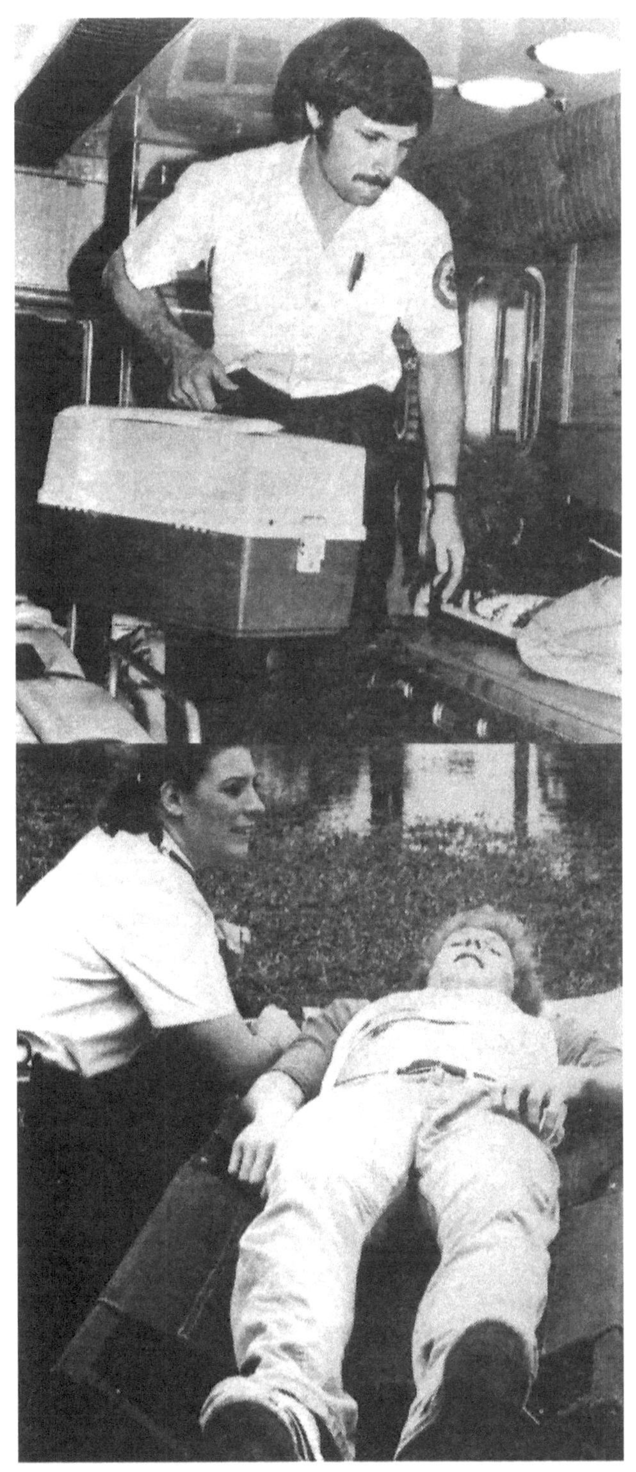

113. Nancy Dougan, representing the Platinum Coast Chapter of Sweet Adelines, presenting a donation to Paramedic Bill Saunders (*Florida Today*, March 9, 1983). With Nancy is her son Billy Murtagth, who was transported by HCVAS after receiving injuries from a motorcycle accident.

114. HCVAS celebrated its 17th anniversary on September 1983 with a cake at its headquarters on Hickory St. Shown at the open house are Doris and Ferd Deserable, Dr. Armstrong and his daughter with members Clare Tyler and Tom Kelly, and Carmen (Dziak) Sanchez and Nicki Ostroff. The squad now had 11 paid paramedics, 8 ambulances, and 1 non-emergency vehicle.

Brevard County

BOARD OF COUNTY COMMISSIONERS

Resolution

WHEREAS, in 1966, seven concerned citizens organized the HARBOR CITY VOLUNTEER AMBULANCE SQUAD to provide emergency ambulance service in South Brevard; and during the past 17 years, the SQUAD increased to over 200 members donating over 100,000 hours of service each year; and

WHEREAS, each member of the SQUAD must have specialized training prior to serving on a crew; more than half of the members are certified Emergency Medical Technicians; and in 1981, with the establishment of the advanced life support system, 11 paid paramedics joined many certified paramedic volunteers; and

WHEREAS, in addition to the main headquarters in Melbourne, satellite stations are located on the South Beaches, in Palm Bay and Eau Gallie, and eight of the nine ambulances are fully equipped for advanced life support emergency medical care; and

WHEREAS, the SQUAD operates primarily by donations, responds to an average of 750 calls each month, provides free emergency medical service and wheelchairs, walkers, crutches and canes on a free-loan basis; and this Board is proud of the SQUAD and desires to commend the volunteers who give their time and skills to help the citizens of South Brevard.

NOW, THEREFORE BE IT RESOLVED, THAT THE BOARD OF COUNTY COMMISSIONERS OF BREVARD COUNTY, FLORIDA, does hereby unanimously recognize and commend

HARBOR CITY VOLUNTEER AMBULANCE SQUAD

for their outstanding performance, genuine concern, and dedicated public service; and extends its congratulations on the celebration of their 17th Anniversary.

DONE, ORDERED AND ADOPTED, in regular session, this ___8th___ day of ___September___ , A.D., 1983.

ATTEST:

R. C. WINSTEAD, JR., CLERK

D. GENE ROBERTS, CHAIRMAN
BOARD OF COUNTY COMMISSIONERS
BREVARD COUNTY, FLORIDA

115. Board of County Commissioners' Resolution celebrating HCVAS' 17 years of service (September 8, 1983).

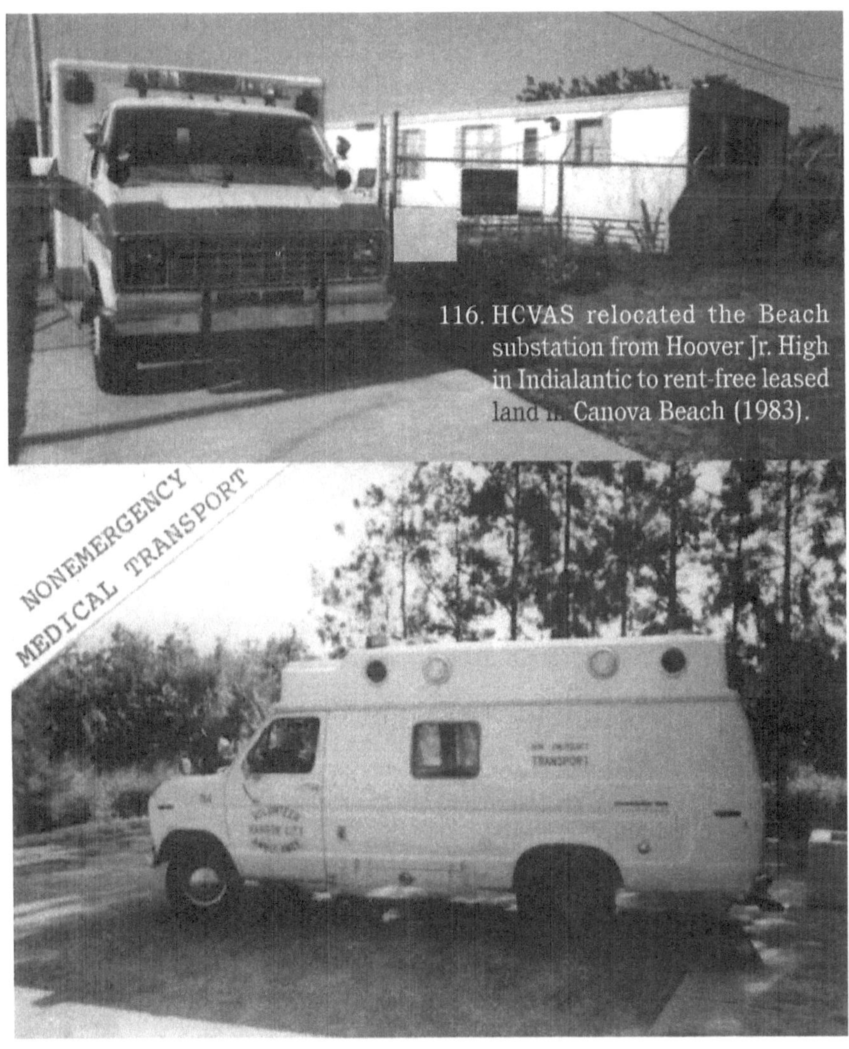

116. HCVAS relocated the Beach substation from Hoover Jr. High in Indialantic to rent-free leased land in Canova Beach (1983).

117. HCVAS' first non-emergency medical transport unit (1984). The unit was used to take patients to doctor appointments, kidney dialysis, etc.

118. An ad in a newspaper soliciting the community for medical and non-medical volunteers.

119. Dispatchers (a) Ann Jones, on left; (b) Edith Koelsch; and (c) Linda Light at the Hickory Street headquarters. Although their primary duty was the prompt dispatching of crews to emergency calls, they also scheduled non-emergency transport calls.

120. Sharon Graham and Pat Chadwick checking out Unit 768 at the Hickory Street headquarters.

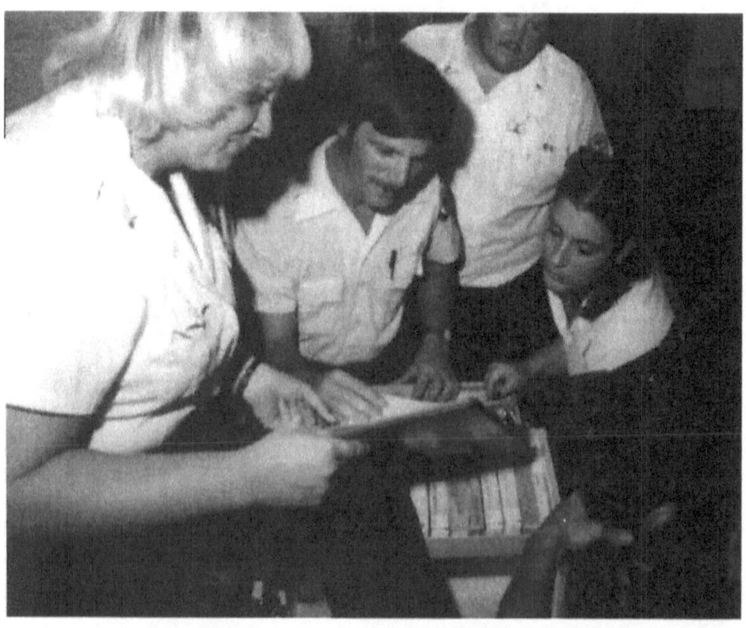

121. Pam Coker, Bill Scholl, Frank Williams, and Vicki Marsden reviewing a run sheet.

122. Annette Smith waiting for a call in the "ready room" at the Hickory Street headquarters.

123. Jill Mitchell, Joe Buehler and Jack Ary ready to take free blood pressures.

124. Barbara Fancher in the dispatch office at the Hickory Street headquarters. Posted is a fund drive "thermometer."

125. Paramedic supervisor Tony Mincu meeting with Indialantic Mayor Andrea Deretany (1984). An agreement was made for HCVAS to staff a three-person crew at the Indialantic fire station. The crew would cover emergency calls from Pinetree Drive to the Aquarina development 15 miles south of Melbourne Beach.

126. Members John Weatherly and Dennis Tyler (HCVAS president 1982-4) in uniform at the dedication of Palm Bay substation on property donated by Harris Government Systems. The move from the old police station in 1984 was aided by contributions from the Palm Bay Rotary Club.

127. Palm Bay substation at its new Clermont Avenue location on land donated by Harris Government Systems (1984). Harris Corp. began matching funds donated to HCVAS.

128. Substation on Aurora Road near Eau Gallie High School. In 1984, HCVAS added this substation because call volume had increased to 12,000 (1500 more than the previous year).

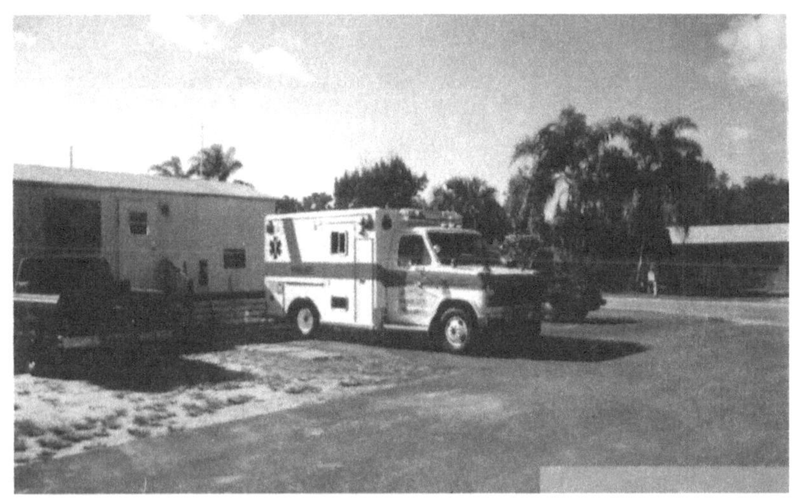

129. Substation in West Melbourne at 90 East Court. Crews that worked at the Hickory Street headquarters were transferred to this facility in 1984. Rapid growth in South Brevard caused traffic congestion on US 192 and Babcock Street. With this new station, crews could respond more quickly to emergency calls in West Palm Bay and West Melbourne. HCVAS had 250 members, 17 paid paramedics, 9 ALS ambulances, and 5 substations. It also began billing patients' insurance companies for services, but it waived the bills of the uninsured.

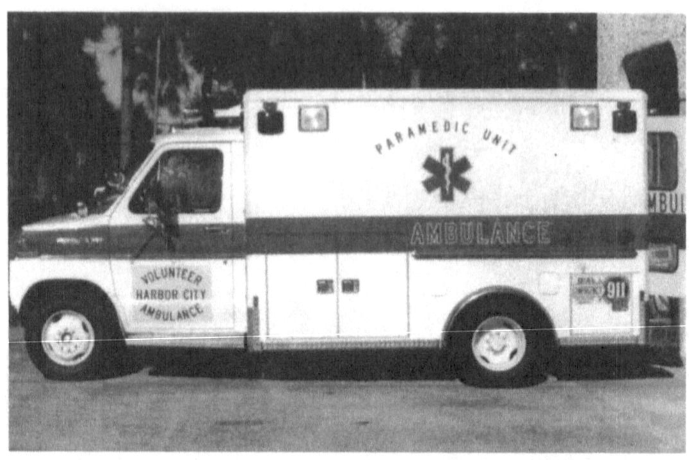

130. Unit 765, a new ALS ambulance, parked in front of a bay at the Hickory Street headquarters. In 1983, HCVAS had collected $275,000 in donations, but by August 1984, only $70,000 had been received. The squad had to dip into a fund set aside for expanding the Hickory Street headquarters to meet expenses.

131. South Melbourne Beach fire station located in the unincorporated area. In November 1984, HCVAS negotiated with county officials to have jurisdiction of the south beaches returned. This would require the county to increase its subsidy to pay for more personnel and equipment.

132. Jay McCarthy holding a "fan" while covering a special event, the General Development Corporation picnic (February 1985).

133. Members on a weekend cruise to the Bahamas.

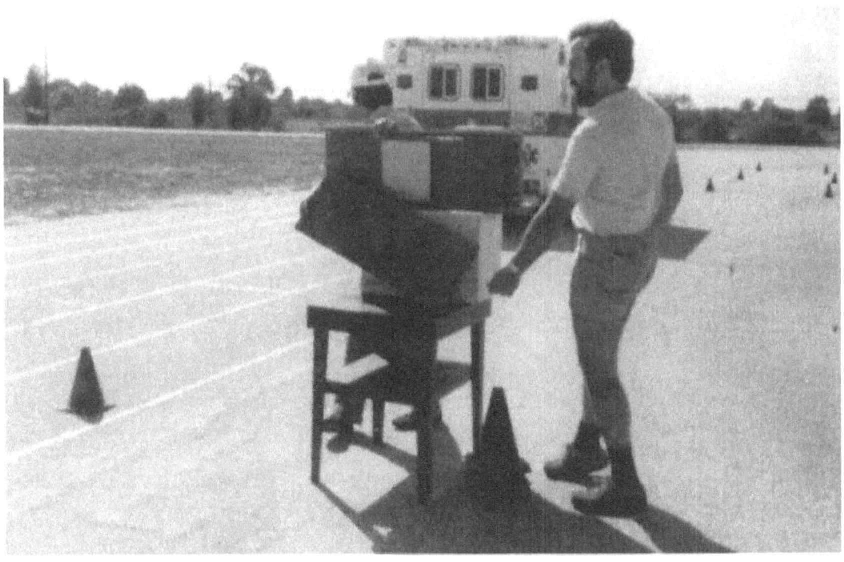

134. Cliff Cooper conducting EVOC (Emergency Vehicle Operator Course) training at Central Jr. High in Melbourne. The class was designed to train members to be ambulance drivers. Each participant had to have a valid Florida license (points free) and a chauffeur's license. Later a Class E endorsement requirement was added.

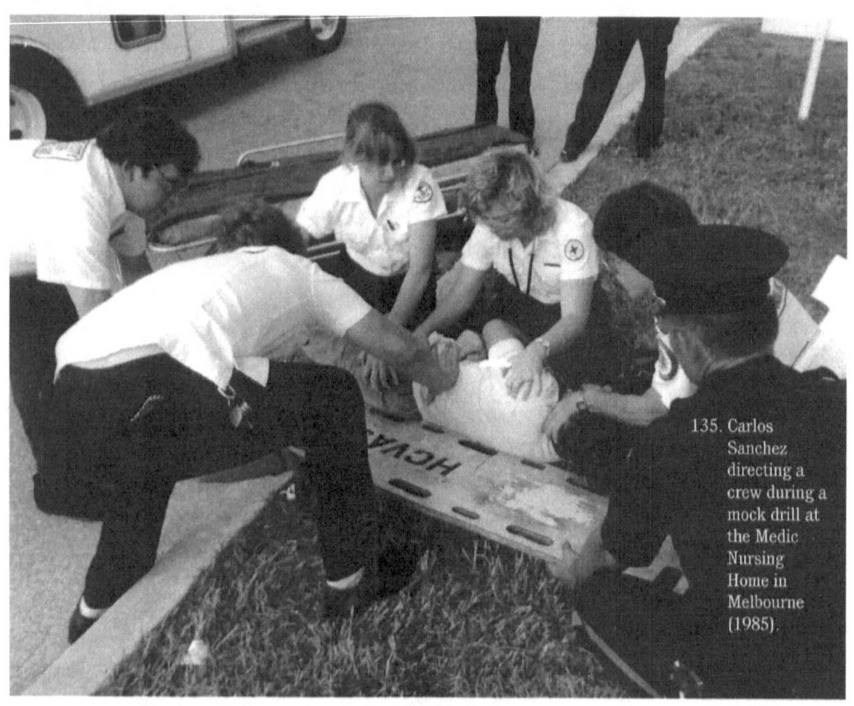

135. Carlos Sanchez directing a crew during a mock drill at the Medic Nursing Home in Melbourne (1985).

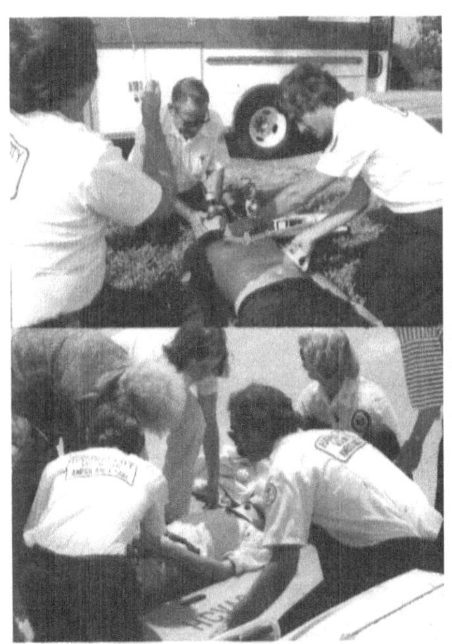

136. More scenes of the mock training drill at Medic Nursing Home in Melbourne (1985). Some of the participants included Lori Ellison, Debbie Ferris, Lonnie Cantor, Ken Rogers, Jim Skidmore, Joel Ostroff, Tom McClenahan, Phil Fahey, and Mike Hunt.

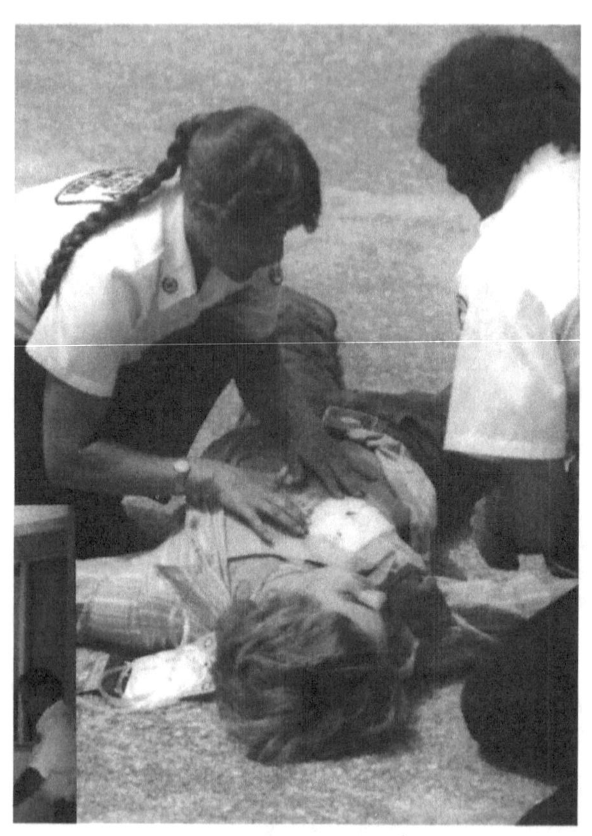

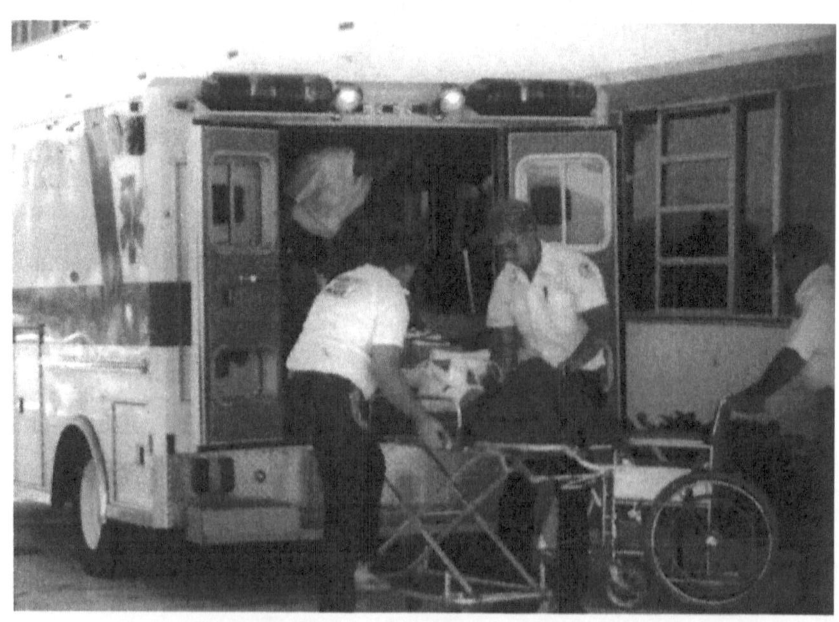

137. Dave Hancock, a mechanic with Brevard County, servicing one of HCVAS' ambulances. Part of the county subsidy included covering the cost of fuel and rig maintenance. Also shown is the County Barn, where ambulances were taken for service.

138. Dennis Tyler (a) and Steve Beyer and Ann Pattalano (b) playing softball at a picnic at Rodes Park, West Melbourne (1986).

139. HCVAS memorabilia: uniform patches, early back patch, jacket, and coffee mug.

License plates and a bumper sticker

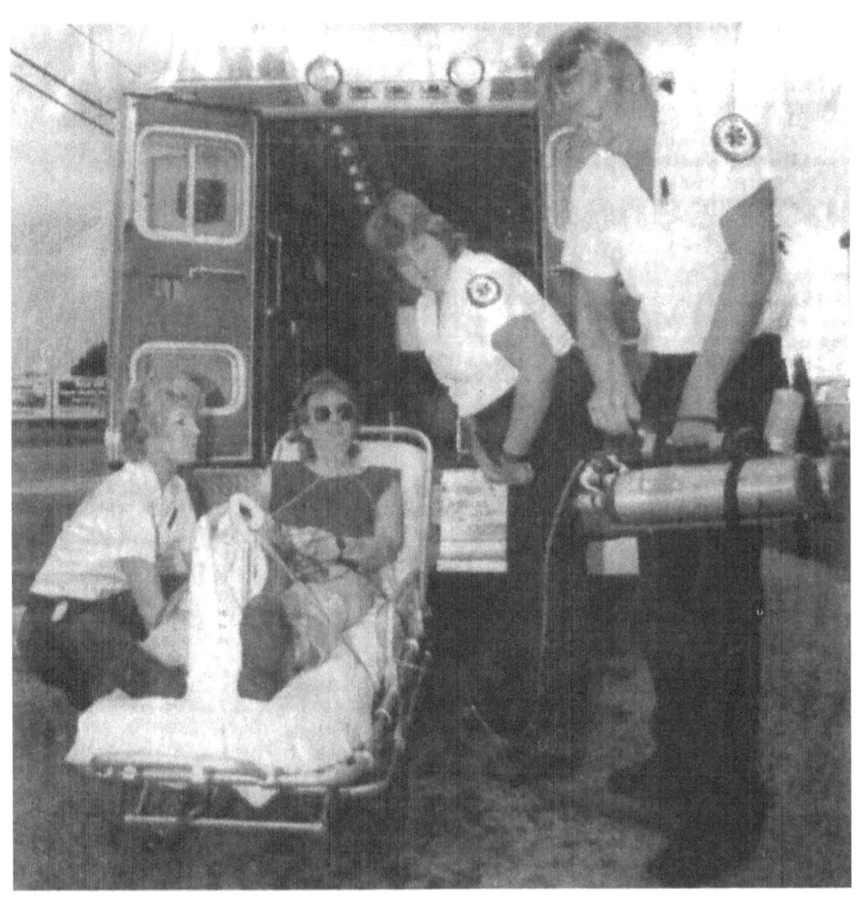

140. Aggie Carlson, Andrea Russell, and Chris Daymude practice loading "patient" Louise Owens (*Florida Today*, May 1986). HCVAS now operated with a budget of over $1,000,000. In 1985, the county contributed $350,000 for expenses, but it cost the squad $800,000 to operate. The difference was made up from donations and reimbursements from patients' insurance companies.

141. Jackie Shipp, Louise Owens (driver), Victoria O'Reilly and Chris Daymude standing next to one HCVAS' 12 ALS units (*EMS Sunshine, Vol 1, No. 2*, May 1986). An ambulance cost about $40,000 plus $30,000 to stock the necessary medical supplies and equipment.

142. HCVAS ambulance fleet in bays at the Hickory Street headquarters (May 1986). At its 20th anniversary, the squad had 6 substations that ran approximately 1200 calls per month with an average response time of 6 minutes.

143. An ad placed in the newspaper celebrating HCVAS' 20th anniversary (1986). With 17 paid paramedics, 12 emergency ambulances, 6 substations, and 256 active members, HCVAS was the largest volunteer ambulance squad in the United States and the only volunteer ALS squad in Florida.

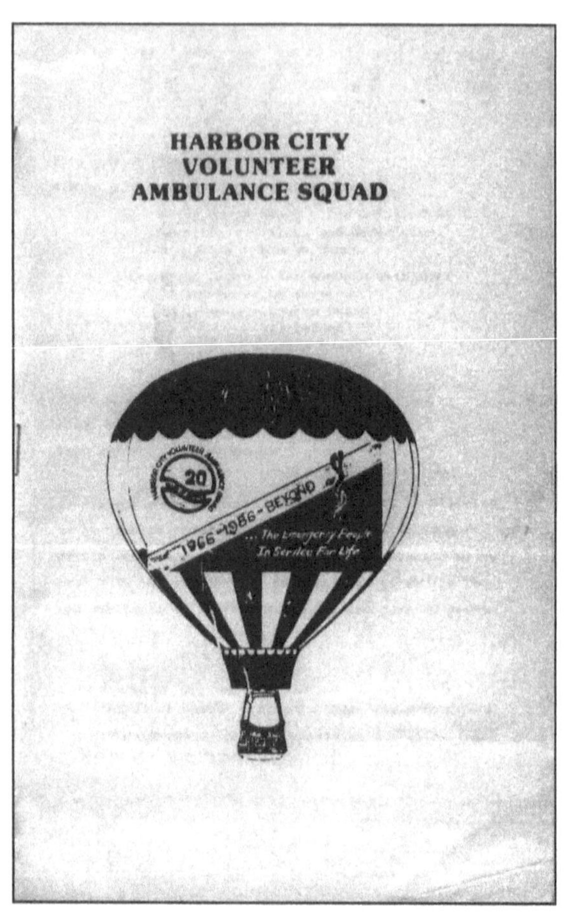

Help Us Help You

Come Help Us Celebrate Our 20th Anniversary

Music by: The American Express & Tuxedo

Hors d'oeuvres   Cash Bar

Melbourne Auditorium
625 E. Hibiscus Blvd., Melbourne

Friday, May 30, 1986
8 P.M. to 1 A.M.

Dress: Semi-formal   Donation $10.00

144. Program and admission ticket for HCVAS' 20th anniversary held May 30, 1986 at the Melbourne Civic Auditorium.

145. Members and guests celebrating HCVAS' 20th anniversary at the Melbourne Civic Auditorium.

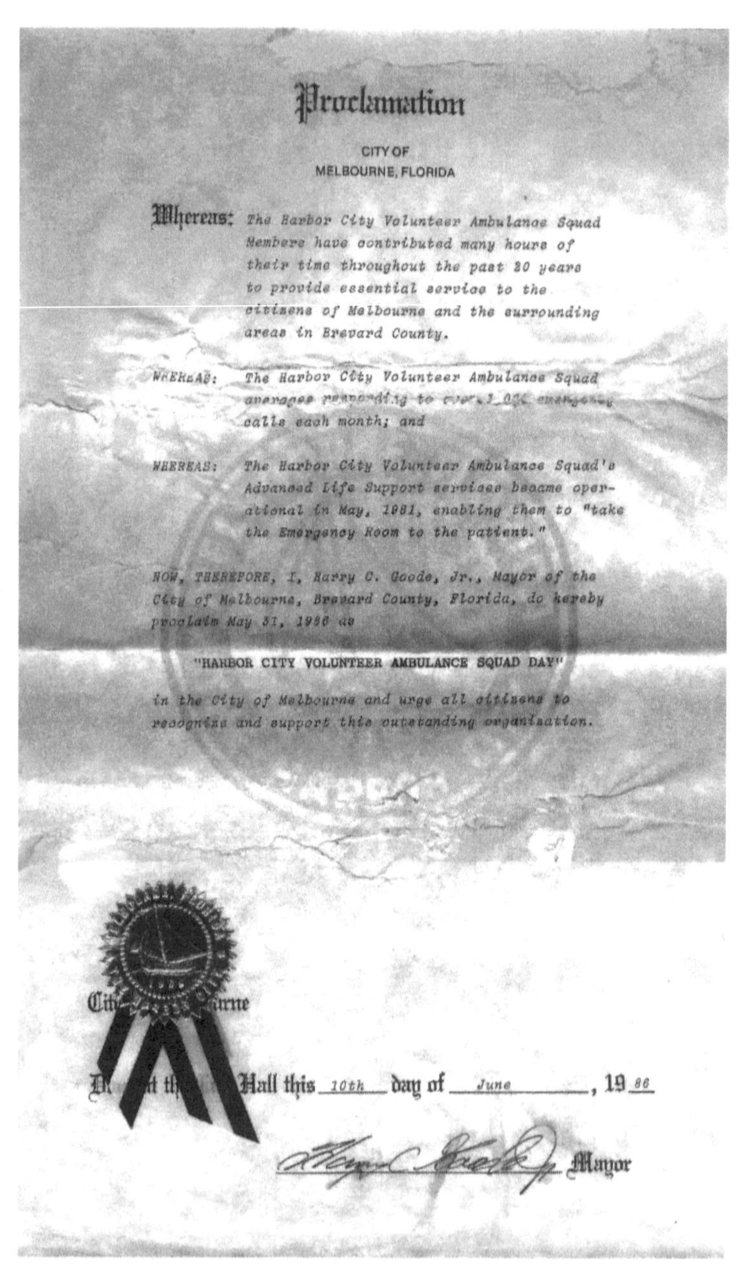

146. Proclamation of the City of Melbourne signed by Mayor Harry Goode, Jr. (June 10, 1986) in honor of HCVAS' 20th anniversary.

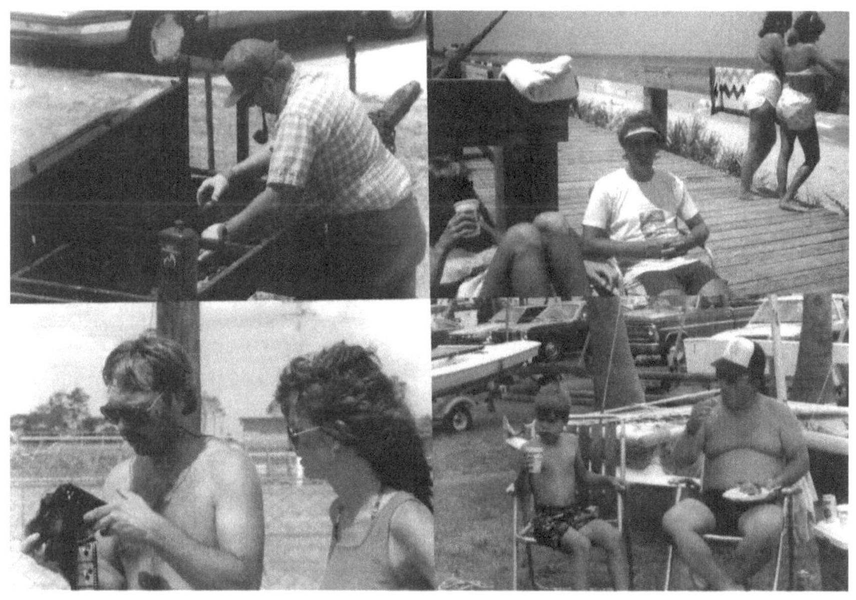

147. Members and guests at a HCVAS picnic held at Spessard Holland Park in Melbourne Beach (1986).

148. An ad placed in the newspaper in 1986, asking for volunteers. Each member had to have at least 40 hours of training in American Red Cross First Aid, CPR, and rig training on ambulance equipment and procedures before riding with the EMTs and paramedics. The squad also had a cadet program that gave high school students the opportunity to see if they would like to make EMS their profession.

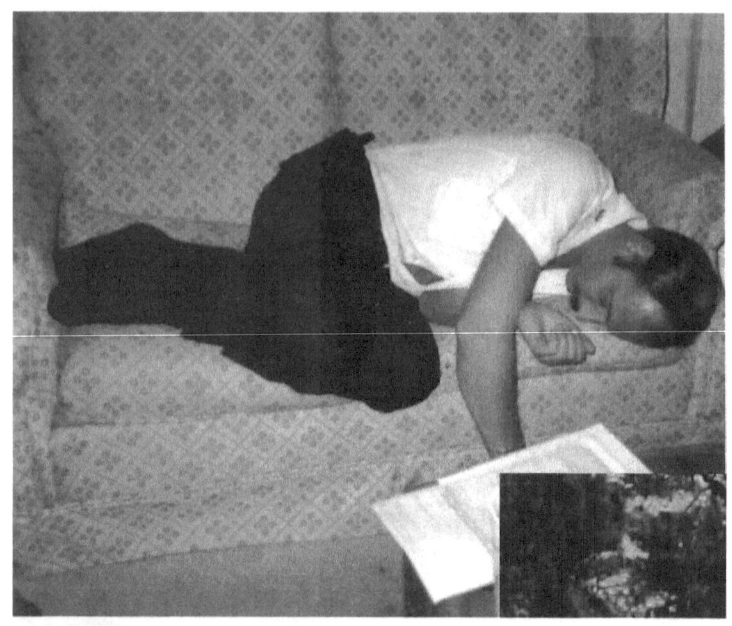

149. When a man died of a heart attack on the Suntree golf course, it took an ambulance 25 minutes to arrive on the scene. Because of this incident, the Suntree Pineda Rotary Club began a fundraiser to place another substation in North Melbourne. Crews began operating out of this station on August 26, 1986. Gardner Whitney is shown napping between calls at the substation.

150. Members shown in costume at a Halloween party.

IV.

Honors and Records 1987-1991

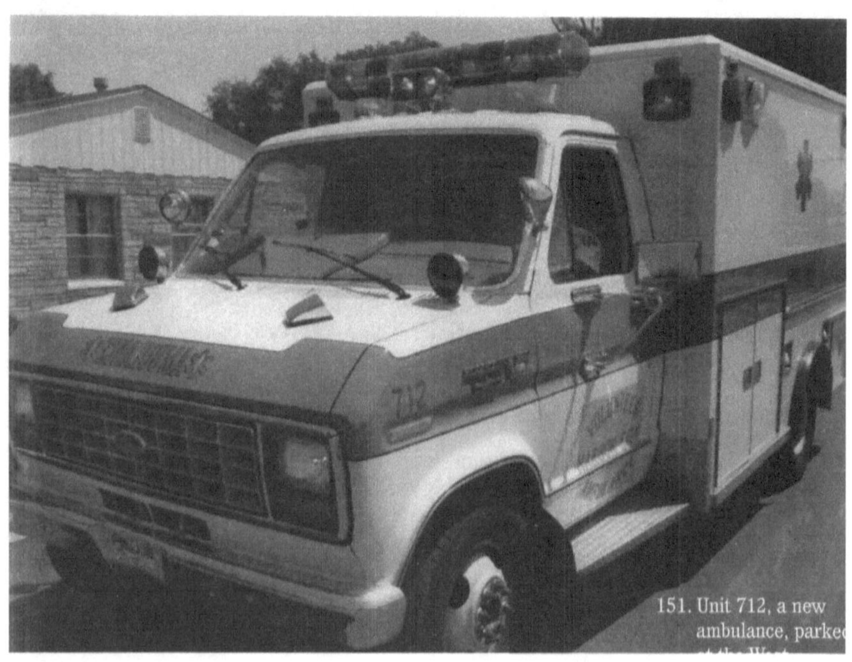

151. Unit 712, a new ambulance, parked at the West Melbourne
substation (1987).

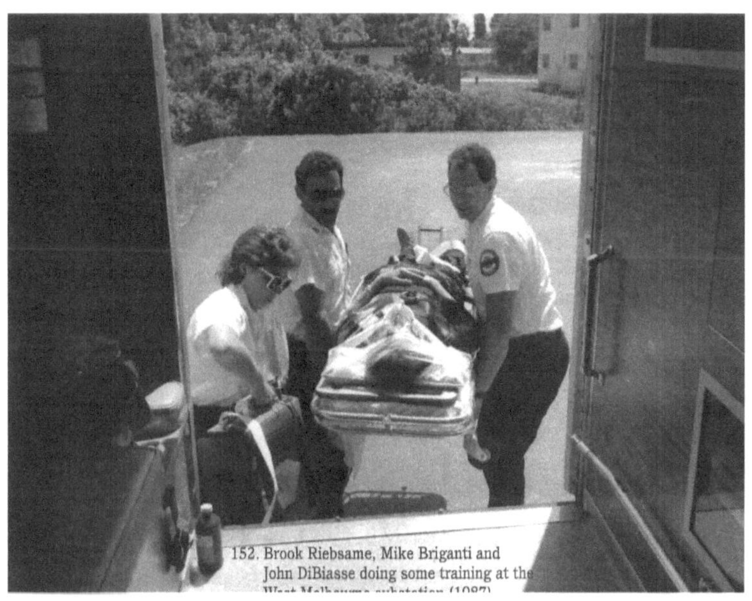

152. Brook Riebsame, Mike Briganti and John DiBiasse doing some training at the West Melbourne substation (1987).

153. On April 23, 1987, William Cruse, a retired librarian, wounded 12 people and killed 6 in Palm Bay, including two police officers, Ronald Grogan and Gerald Johnson (*Florida Today*, April 24, 1987). Mike Wise, a HCVAS paramedic, was wounded when his ambulance (Unit 766) was hit by several bullets. The other crew members were Dave Hubbard and Jim Skidmore.

Cruse's victims

Enad Al-Tawakuly

Al-Tawakuly

Al-Tawakuly, 18, had been enrolled at Florida Tech less than one month when he was gunned down outside Publix. He was shot in the upper leg and left side. Bullets pierced his lungs.

Nobil Al-Hameli

Al-Hameli, 25, was shot in the back, shoulder, stomach and hand as he walked out of Publix. He was a roommate of Al-Tawakuly.

Al-Hameli

Ruth Greene

Greene

Greene, 67, lived in Palm Bay for 23 years. She was shot in the head and side as she tried to drive away from Publix. She had stopped at the store to buy lettuce for her guinea pig.

Gerald Johnson

Johnson, 28, a Palm Bay police officer, was shot in the leg, arm and chest. As Johnson tried to reload his six-shot revolver, Cruse came up behind him and shot him. He died on the scene.

Johnson

Ron Grogan

Grogan

Grogan, 27, also a Palm Bay police officer, was shot at least eight times in the head and chest. Grogan was a 1978 graduate of Satellite High. He was married only two months before his death.

Lester Watson

Watson, 52, was shot in the back as he was trying to flee Winn-Dixie. A Syracuse, N.Y., native, Watson was married with four children, Kevin, Andrew, Leslie and Eric.

Watson

154. Cruse's victims are ahown in *Florida Today*, April 23, 2002, and William Cruse at a court appearance on December 15, 1987. This incident severely tested a new disaster plan, and the physicians and medical community proved the plan worked (*FMA, Florida Medical Association, Inc., Vol III*, No. 5, May 1987.

155. In May 1987, Governor Bob Martinez honored 15 people during Palm Bay Heroes Day in Tallahassee (*Orlando Sentinel*, May 8, 1987). Mike Wise, Jim Skidmore and Dave Hubbard were honored for removing wounded residents from the Winn-Dixie grocery store parking lot while the gunman sprayed them with bullets. Tom and Christine Adler were honored for rescuing several injured residents under gunfire.

Proclamation
City of Palm Bay, Florida

NOTICE AND PROCLAMATION OF

IN RECOGNITION OF

HARBOR CITY VOLUNTEER AMBULANCE SQUAD

IT IS HEREBY PROCLAIMED BY THE MAYOR OF THE CITY OF PALM BAY, BREVARD COUNTY, FLORIDA, that:

WHEREAS, on April 23, 1987, a lone gunman suddenly and without provocation opened fire at the Sabal Palm Shopping Plaza; and

WHEREAS, this malicious and deliberate act resulted in the deaths and injuries of innocent civilians and law enforcement personnel; and

WHEREAS, the HARBOR CITY VOLUNTEER AMBULANCE SQUAD responded to a call for assistance and subsequently performed in an outstanding manner in the face of imminent death or great bodily harm; and

WHEREAS, the agency's personnel performed in a highly professional manner under extraordinarily difficult circumstances, while making every possible effort to protect and defend innocent citizens from the gunman's fire.

NOW, THEREFORE, I, Harold F. Bryant, Sr., Mayor of the City of Palm Bay, by virtue of the authority of said office, do hereby recognize and honor the

HARBOR CITY VOLUNTEER AMBULANCE SQUAD

and call upon all citizens and fellow police officers and personnel in joining me in paying tribute to the HARBOR CITY VOLUNTEER AMBULANCE SQUAD for their unselfish act and devotion to duty which has brought credit to their agency and the entire police profession.

IN WITNESS WHEREOF, I have hereunto set my hand and caused the Seal of the City of Palm Bay to be affixed this Eleventh day of June, Nineteen Hundred Eighty-Seven.

Harold F. Bryant, Sr., MAYOR

ATTEST:

Alice Passmore, CITY CLERK

156. Proclamation by the City of Palm Bay signed by mayor Harold F. Bryant (June 11, 1987) honoring the HCVAS response to the April 23, 1987 incident.

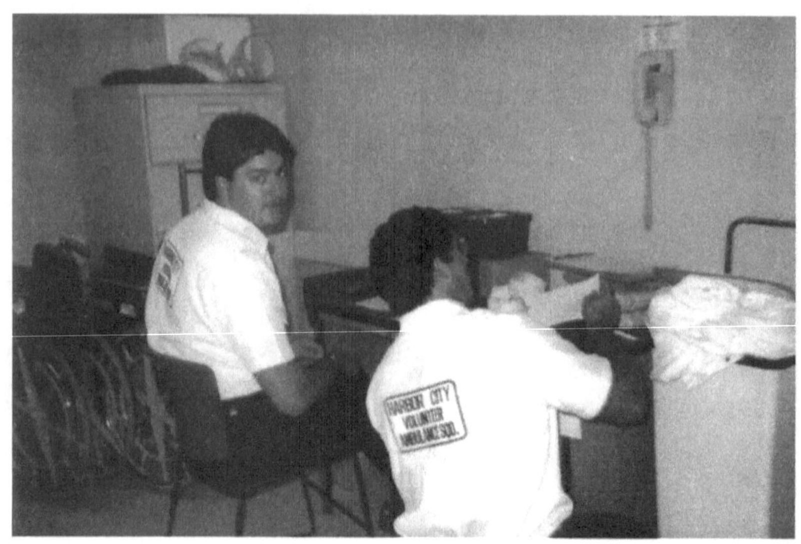

157. Carl Loveridge and Mike Wise finishing their paper work in the ER (Holmes Regional Medical Center) after running an ambulance call.

158. In June 1987, HCVAS relocated the crew stationed at the Indialantic fire station to a substation behind the Melbourne Beach Town Hall on Ocean Avenue (shown is a newer mobile home that replaced the original).

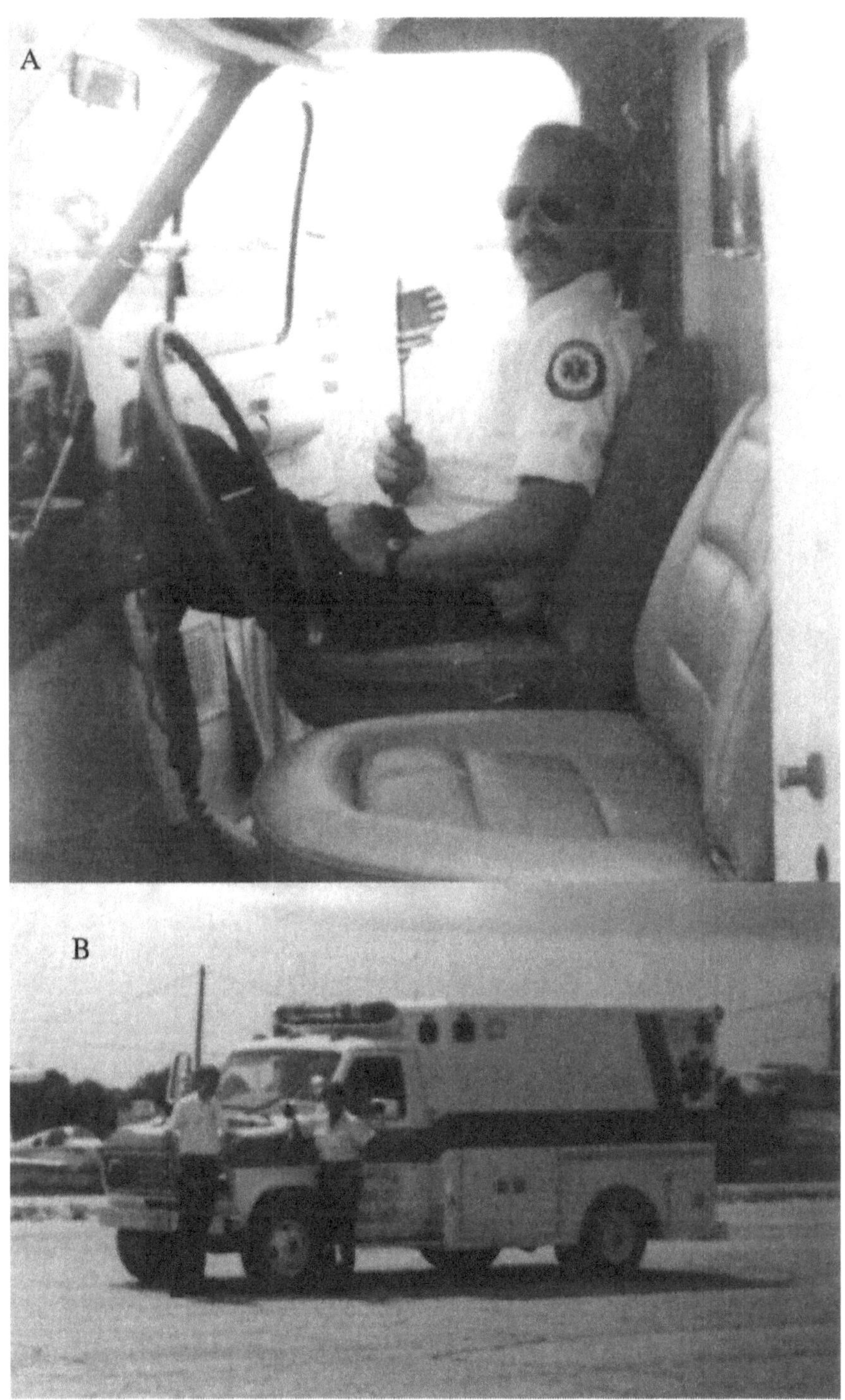

159. HCVAS crew Lennie Asher (a) and Carlos Sanchez and Debbie
Buckley (b) providing medical stand-by coverage when President
Ronald Reagan visited Melbourne on August 3, 1987. Air Force
1 (c & d) is shown parked at Melbourne International Airport.

August 3, 1987

Dear Mr. Hunt:

I want to thank you for all you did in connection with my trip to Melbourne. I know how much hard work goes into making a Presidential visit successful. You have my heartfelt appreciation for a job well done.

Nancy joins me in sending our very best wishes. God bless you.

Sincerely,

Ronald Reagan

Mr. Mike Hunt
Harbor City Volunteer
   Ambulance Squad
1131 South Hickory Street
Melbourne, Florida   32901

160. Copy of a letter (August 3, 1987) that President Ronald Reagan sent to Mike Hunt. Each of the HCVAS members who provided medical stand-by coverage for the President's visit to Melbourne received a similar "thank-you" letter.

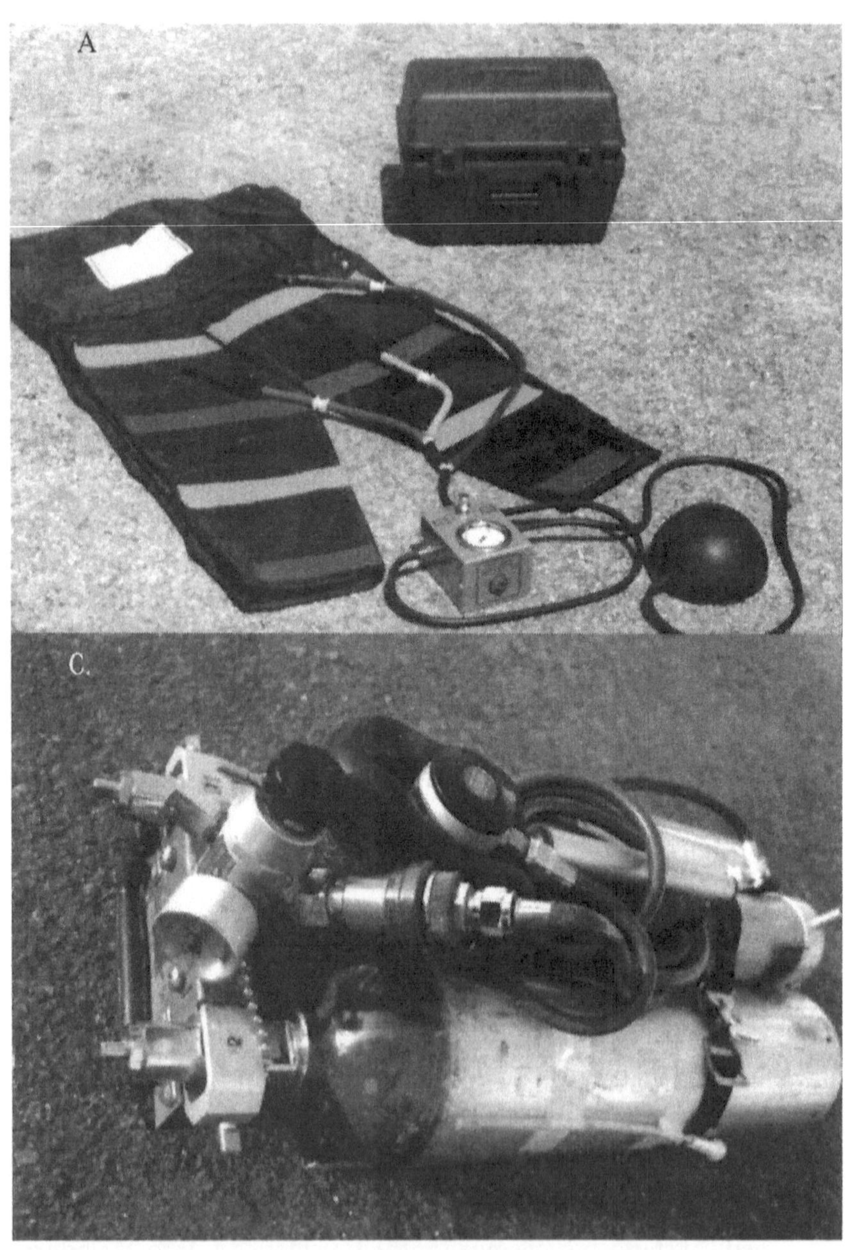

A
C.

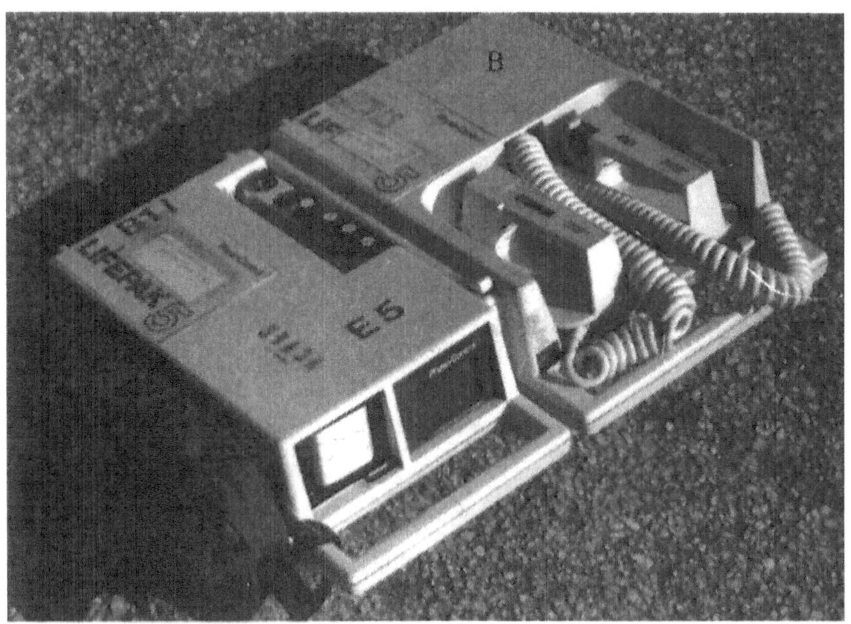

161. Some of the equipment used on the ambulances in 1987 included (a) MAST suit, (b) LifePak 5, and (c) portable oxygen.

In 1987, the squad had 250 volunteers, 30 paid paramedics and answered on the average 1600 calls per month.

162. Flyer advertising the CPR (cardiopulmonary resuscitation) "Awareness" Marathon held at the Melbourne Square Mall from January 1-3, 1988.

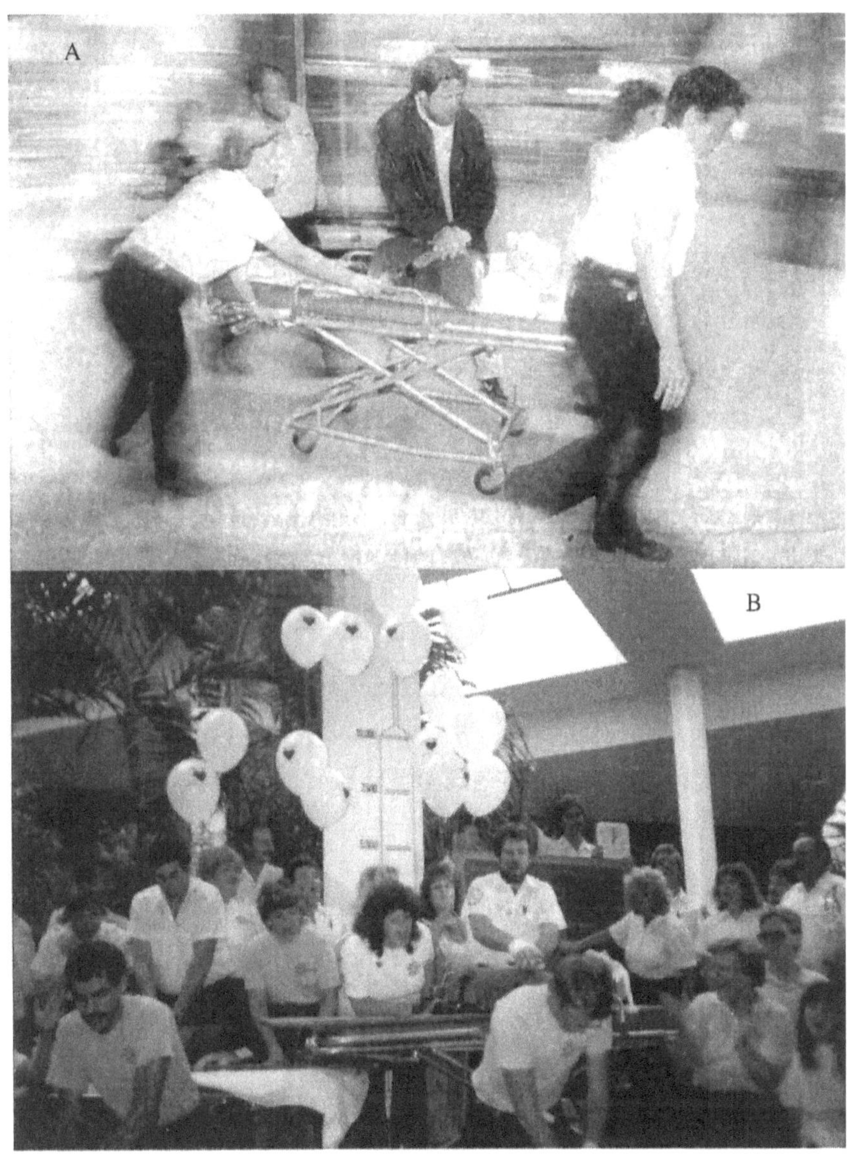

A
B

163. Frank Blake (a) performing CPR on a manikin while the staff moved the stretcher from the ambulance into the Melbourne Square Mall courtyard (*Florida Today*, January 2, 1988). The 77-hour CPR marathon began at the Hickory Street headquarters on December 31, 1987 and moved to the mall on January 1, 1988. Two 2-man teams (Kevin McKowen & Frank Blake; Les Williams & David Baily) participated in the marathon (b). They performed continuous CPR from noon Thursday to 5:00 pm Sunday and beat the world record of 73 hours set by Geoff Law and Frank Smith of West Midlands Ambulance Service in Birmingham, AL. Debbie Gaffney (c) shown with Frank Blake helped officiate at the event.

164. Shown at the CPR marathon are (a) Sharon Irvin and Mike Hunt answering questions, (b) Mark and Kim Callahan (co-director) taking a break, and (c) Carlos Sanchez taking blood pressures. Members gave lessons to children on dialing 911 in emergencies and encouraged the public to sign up for CPR and first aid classes. The event also included a membership drive for office personnel, ambulance attendants, non-emergency transport personnel, and dispatchers. It took approximately 538 man-hours each day to staff all of HCVAS' substations.

**Congress
of the
United States
House of Representatives**

BILL NELSON
FLORIDA
ELEVENTH DISTRICT

CHAIRMAN OF SUBCOMMITTEE
SPACE SCIENCE AND APPLICATIONS
COMMITTEES:
SCIENCE, SPACE AND TECHNOLOGY
BANKING, FINANCE AND URBAN AFFAIRS

January 8, 1988

Harbor City Vol. Ambulance Squad
1131 South Hickory Street
Melbourne, Florida 32901

Dear Friends:

Congratulations on setting the two, two-man-team record for performing CPR, and thereby gaining considerable good public relations for CPR and HCVAS.

This is an outstanding tribute to your accomplishment. Best wishes for continued success.

Please contact me any time I may be of service. Kind personal regards.

Sincerely,

Bill Nelson

IN RESPONSE, PLEASE REPLY TO:

WASHINGTON OFFICE
2404 RAYBURN HOUSE OFFICE BUILDING
WASHINGTON, D.C. 20515-0912
(202) 225-3671

MELBOURNE OFFICE
780 SOUTH APOLLO BLVD., SUITE 12
MELBOURNE, FLORIDA 32901-1423
(305) 676-1776

ORLANDO OFFICE
FEDERAL BUILDING, SUITE 300
ORLANDO, FLORIDA 32801-2225
(305) 841-1776

KISSIMMEE OFFICE (305) 847-1280
MERRITT ISLAND OFFICE (305) 453-9524
TITUSVILLE OFFICE (305) 268-1776
VERO BEACH OFFICE (305) 589-1978

165. Letter dated January 8, 1988 from Congressman Bill Nelson, congratulating the two CPR marathon teams.

166. When a British team beat HCVAS' record in January 1988, the teams reclaimed the world record and were listed in the Guinness Book of World Records. Three 2-man teams (Les Williams & David Baily; Angie Drinkard & Rich Martel; and Sheri Johnson & Michelle Tyler) did the 120-hour marathon at the Melbourne Beach Hilton from September 1-6, 1988. Shown are (a) Michelle Tyler, Angie Drinkard, and Les Williams with their hands wrapped to protect them in the grueling event and (b) Commissioner Thad Altman cheering-on Michelle and Angie. At the marathon, the community could tour ambulances, sign up for CPR classes, and learn how to become a HCVAS volunteer. On September 6, an auction was held at 7:00 pm at the Hilton to help defer costs of the event. About 25 nurses, firefighters and paramedics were "auctioned off" as dates for an evening of dinner and drinks aboard an Indian River paddleboat.

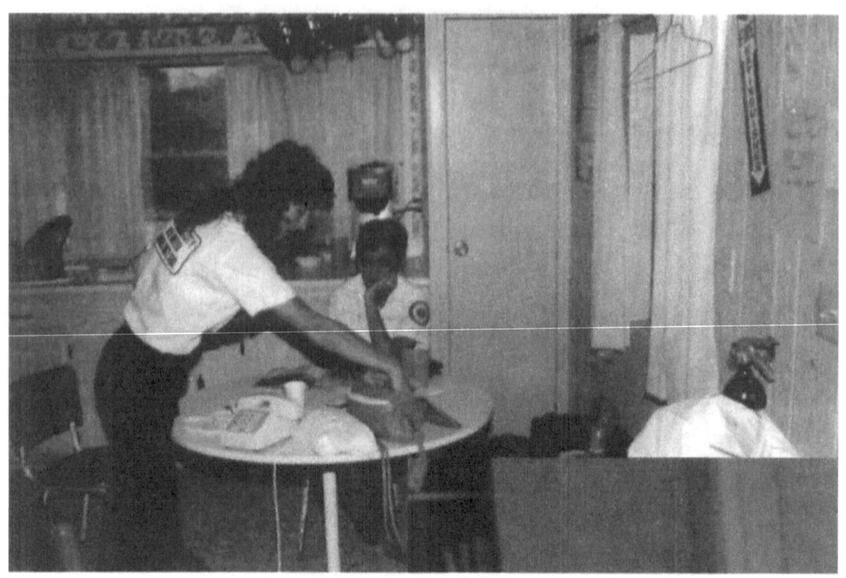

167. Sue McCuiston and Debbie Buckley on duty at the Canova Beach substation. In 1988, HCVAS renumbered its ambulance stations, using the 100 series as part of a countywide emergency services plan.

168. Tim Phalen, Director of Operations, at work at the Hickory Street headquarters.

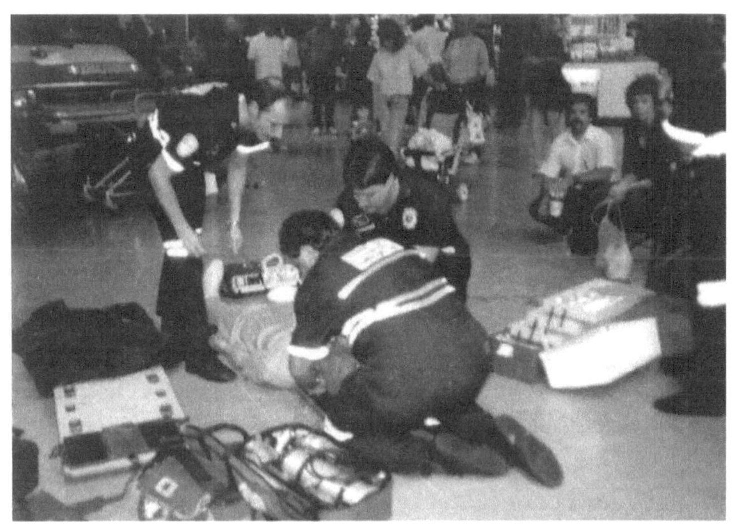

169. HCVAS' ALS competition team (Gardner Whitney, Carl Loveridge, Mike Lodge, and Tim Phalen) doing a demonstration at the Melbourne Square Mall. In 1989, the team placed 14th at Clincon (Clinical Conference), an international EMS competition held annually near Orlando, FL.

170. The old YMCA on Eau Gallie Boulevard in Melbourne. In 1989, the HCVAS Foundation bought the building for insurance and administrative offices. It sold the building in 1995 when renovations proved to be too costly. In 1989, HCVAS had over 200 active volunteers who each donated on the average 42 hours per month.

171. Bill Hoskovec, Director of Operations, handing the keys of the new District 100 vehicle to Mike Hunt (1989). The three field supervisors (Mike Hunt, John DiBiasse, and Chris Bedard) used the vehicle as a "first response truck." The squad also converted its underground fuel tank to diesel.

172. Charlie McCown (paramedic intern), Dagmar Summers (paramedic), and Bill Petrik (driver/attendant) standing in front of the Palm Bay substation, one of HCVAS' busiest stations (*Florida Today*, 1989). Starting salary for a paramedic at this time was $15,500.

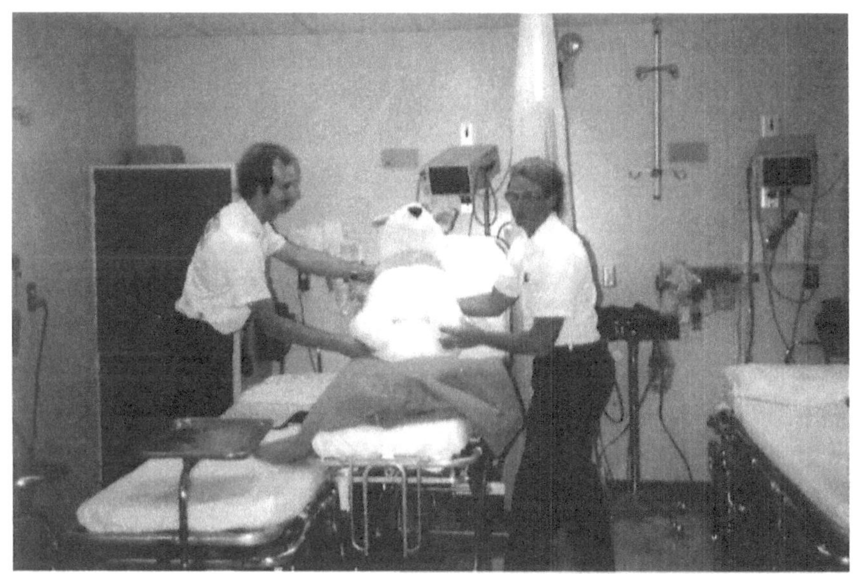

173. Jim Wilson and Les Williams delivering a "patient" to the
    ER. All field personnel were now required to take an AIDS
    Awareness class given by Holmes Regional Medical Center.

174. Jim Turner, a military retiree, dispatching and Mark Carney
    taking a break in the dispatch office.

175. In 1989, HCVAS issued color-coded
ID badges to members. Shown is Jim
Irvin's EMT/driver badge.

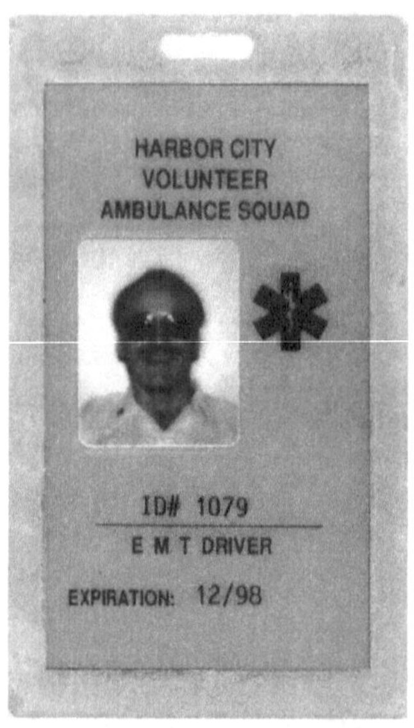

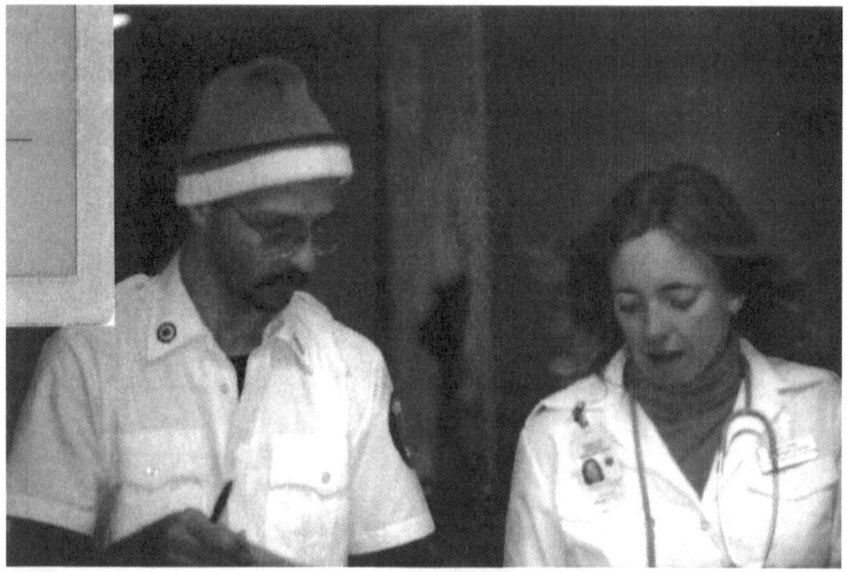

176. Dave Segona and Pat Cornwell discussing an ambulance run
report after delivering a patient to the ER at Holmes Regional
Medical Center.

177. Members and guests at a hot tub party and a "toga" party.

178. Members at a HCVAS picnic at Ryckman Park in Melbourne Beach (1990). The squad had 216 active members (23 volunteer paramedics and 99 EMTs), 40 paid paramedics, 13 ALS vehicles, and 7 satellite stations. It operated on a budget of $2.5 million (30% from county subsidies; 20% from public donations; and 50% from grants, corporate donations and insurance payments). Also in 1990, the squad replaced the Lifepak 5 cardiac heart monitors with Lifepak 10s.

179. In 1991, HCVAS relocated the Malabar substation from the
42 acres owned by HRMC to the Malabar fire station when a
120-bed hospital went under construction.

New "sunburst" back patch

180. Barbara Keesing, a volunteer EMT, ready to take the driver's
seat. In 1991, HCVAS established its "no smoking" and "sexual
harassment" policies and adopted the new "sun burst" back
patch for members' uniforms.

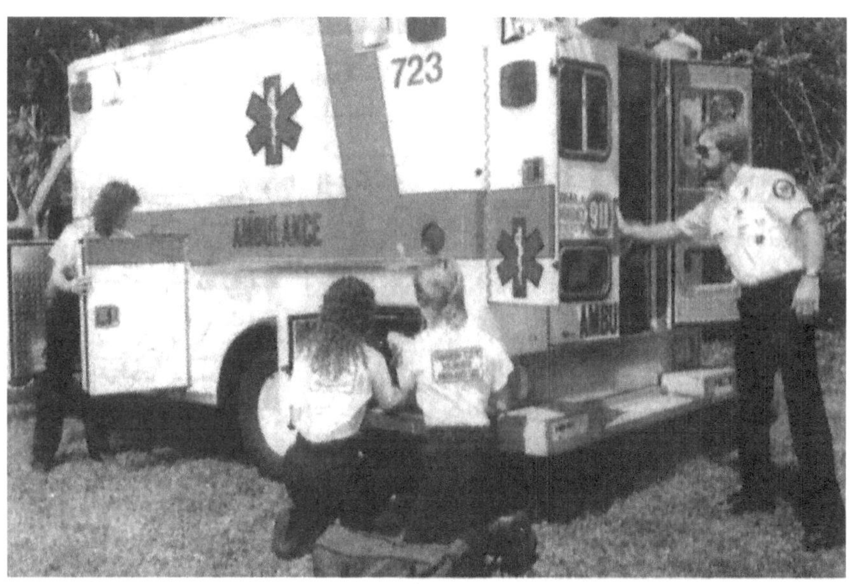

181. Sue McCuiston, Ed Clemons and their crew checking out the vehicle for another day (*Orlando Sentinel*, May 24, 1991). In 1991, HCVAS had 7 substations and 18 ambulances. Besides ALS and non-emergency transports, HCVAS offered standard first aid, CPR, and EMT refresher classes.

182. Members posing in front the Hickory Street headquarters for HCVAS' 25th anniversary (*Florida Today*, May 1991). A catered dinner with entertainment provided by the Brevard Symphony Orchestra was held at the Melbourne Civic Center on May 25, 1991 to celebrate the squad's silver anniversary.

Proclamation

Whereas: The Harbor City Volunteer Ambulance Squad, Inc. (HCVAS) will celebrate its Silver Anniversary in May, 1991; and

WHEREAS: HCVAS serves all the communities in South Brevard but calls Melbourne its "homebase" because Melbourne City officials approved HCVAS's initial plans in 1966; and

WHEREAS: HCVAS began with seven volunteer members and a 1961 ambulance purchased for $125. The Squad currently boasts over 350 volunteer members who provide Advanced and Basic Life Support, Standard First Aid, CPR and Emergency Medical Technician refresher courses; and

WHEREAS: HCVAS's versatility is evidenced by its 1990 service record; the Squad responded to over 22,325 calls; and

WHEREAS: The HCVAS responds to all official requests for emergency ambulance and/or medical services from accredited sources, regardless of the individuals' ability to pay for the services.

NOW, THEREFORE, BE IT RESOLVED THAT THE CITY COUNCIL OF THE CITY OF MELBOURNE, BREVARD COUNTY, FLORIDA, does hereby proclaim May 25, 1991 as

"HARBOR CITY AMBULANCE SQUAD SILVER ANNIVERSARY DAY"

in recognition of the Squad's excellent service and dedication provided to our citizens over the past 25 years.

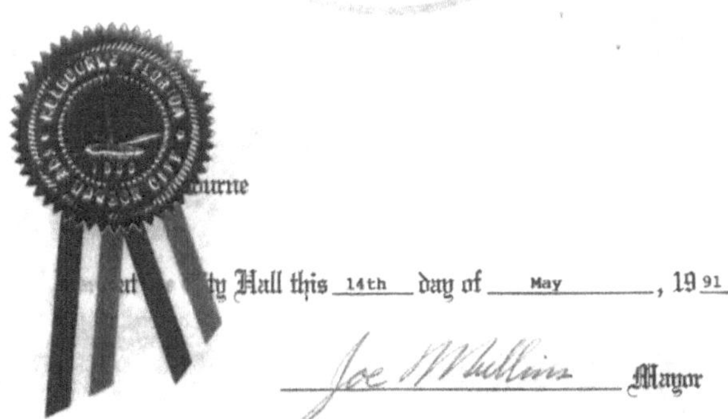

…urne

…at …ty Hall this __14th__ day of ____May____, 19 __91__

________________________ Mayor

183. Proclamation of the City of Melbourne signed by Mayor Joe Mullins (May 14, 1991), honoring HCVAS' 25th anniversary. The squad had 249 active volunteers who each donated on the average 44 hours per month. It responded to about 1500 calls a month (a total of 22,325 calls in 1990) and served South Brevard with a population of 300,000.

184. Copy of an invitation, matchbook cover and program for
HCVAS' 25th anniversary held May 25, 1991 at the Melbourne
Civic Center. About 250 members and guests attended,
including John Clarkson, one of the squad's founders.

25th
Welcome To
Harbor City Volunteer
Ambulance Squad
Silver Anniversary
Party

185. Members and guests celebrating HCVAS' 25th anniversary at the Melbourne Civic Auditorium (1991).

V.

Closure and Legacy 1992-2001

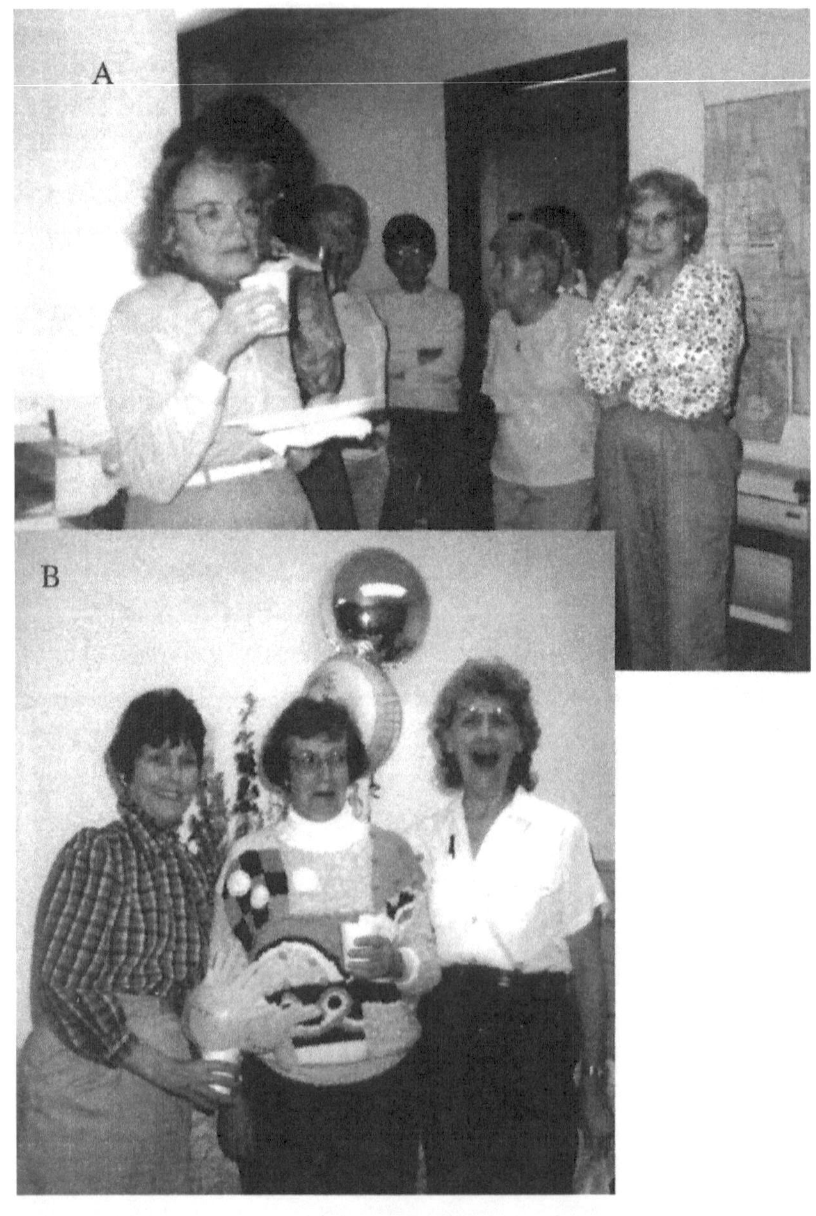

186. Mary Landfried's "going-away" party (February 1992). Those attending included (a) Helen Sherman and June Bracken; (b) Diane McCauley and JoAnn Christie with Mary Landfried in the center; and (c) Pat Vaillancourt and Sandy Coulter. Starting out as a volunteer, Mary resigned from the squad in 1985 to return to college to get a degree in business. She was a member for 18 years and served as HCVAS' second administrative supervisor from 1987 to 1992.

187. Lonnie Cantor, paramedic and member of HRMC's flight team, and Dave Segona, paramedic, at a special event. In 1992, the squad had 249 active volunteers who each donated on the average 40 hours a month.

188. Two of HCVAS' ALS competition teams (*Florida Today*, August 5, 1992). Out of 62 teams at Clincon in July 1992, Carl Loveridge and Dave Segona placed 26th and Les Williams, Butch Williams, and John Arnold placed 7th. All field members now received the Hepatitis B vaccine series and took classes in AIDS Awareness, Bloodborne Pathogens and HazMat Level 1. Also in 1992, ALS units began carrying pulse oximeters.

189. In May 1993, the accounting and insurance offices moved from (a) Nasa Boulevard to (b) Waverly Place. In 1992, HCVAS had begun billing patients for its services aggressively three times in order to be compliant with Medicare regulations.

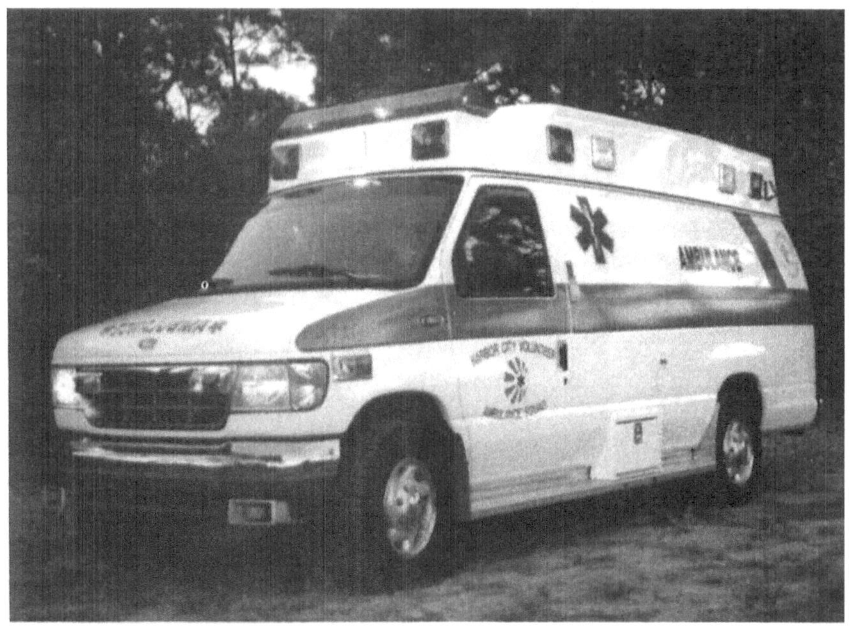

190. In June 1993, HCVAS bought three vans (shown is a later van) for basic life support transports (BLS). It also bought four lift-equipped vans for wheelchair transports that began in October. The squad had 255 active volunteers who each donated on the average 42 hours a month. The basic charge for an ALS call was $250.00.

191. In September 1993, Cliff Cooper (HCVAS president) with Paul Gougleman (HCVAS attorney) signed the papers to purchase property on Minton Road to build another substation in Palm Bay. HCVAS bought this land through the assistance of the State of Florida HRS Department of EMS Matching Fund Grant. In October, the squad adopted the new State EMS run report.

192. In March 1994, HCVAS replaced the mobile home at the substation in Melbourne Beach.

193. Kevin Nelson, HCVAS Public Relations Officer, with Dr. Jane Tolbert, a professor at Florida Institute of Technology. Her Public Relations class designed a PR package for HCVAS (March 1994). Dr. Tolbert is holding a plaque which HCVAS gave the Humanities Department.

194. Scott Schein, Non-Emergency Transports Supervisor, hosting a group of foreign exchange students at the Hickory Street headquarters (April 1994).

195. This article appeared in *Florida Today* on April 22, 1994. John Doty received the J. C. Penney Golden Rule Award for developing and implementing the Wheelchair Transportation Division at HCVAS. John was later featured in the Fall 1994 edition of *The Florida EMS Newsletter* for his groundbreaking work in becoming an EMT in spite of his disability (August 1994).

196. On May 12, 1994, the Palm Bay substation on Minton Road went into service at 11:47 pm, and the crew responded to its first call at 12:20 am. When HCVAS dedicated the substation on June 15, 1994, the keynote speaker was Mike Williams (Director of EMS for the State of Florida). Other dignitaries attending included Mel Broom (Mayor of Palm Bay), Rick Conners (Palm Bay City Councilman), and Pat Poole (Melbourne City Councilwoman).

197. In May 1994, the administration unveiled an architectural
     design for expanding the Hickory Street headquarters (including
     the property directly behind the squad that the Foundation
     bought). HCVAS also formed a parliamentary review committee
     chaired by Jim Irvin to update the organization's Articles of
     Incorporation and bylaws. In July, members approved the new
     bylaws.

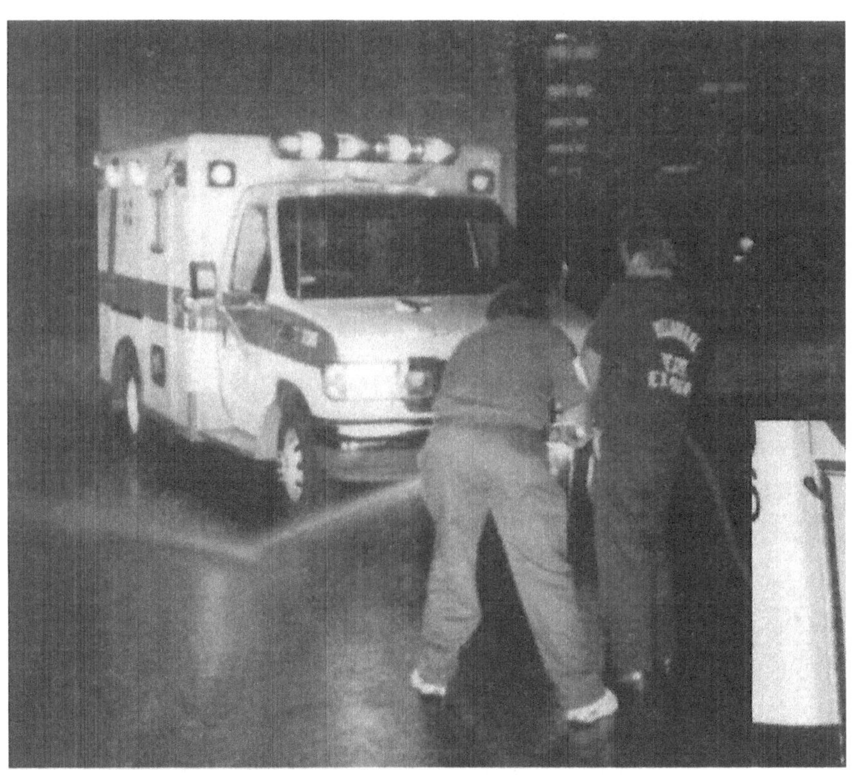

198. Hosing down the pavement in front of the Melbourne Civic Auditorium for a HCVAS public relations photo shoot.

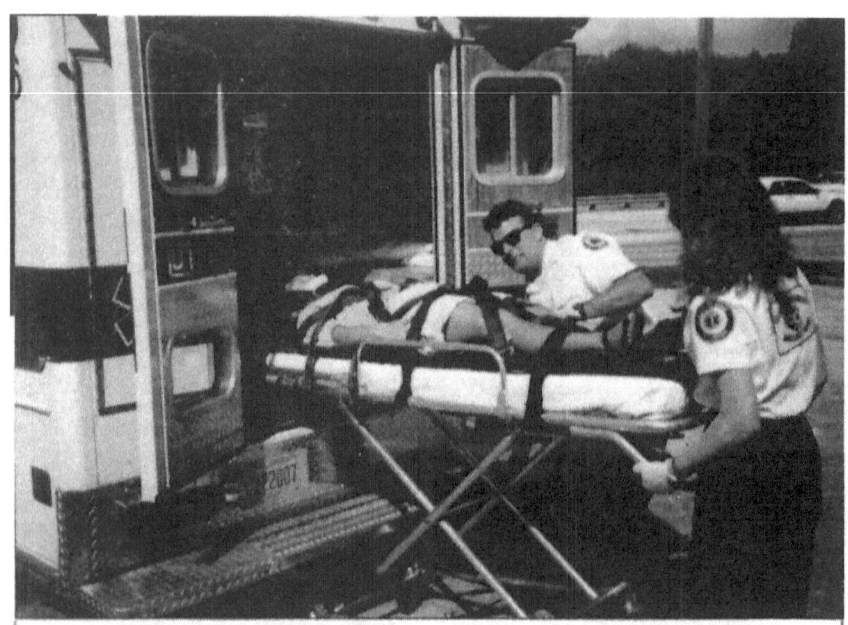

199. Dave Geer and Sue McCuiston pictured on a flyer soliciting the community for more volunteers.

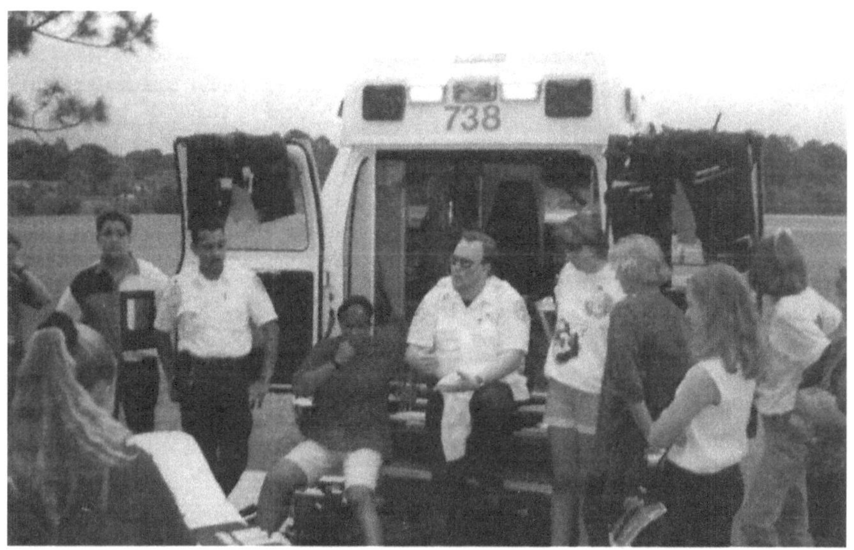

200. David Rodriguez-Wells-Torres and Mike Dalton explaining the
role of EMS to students at a HCVAS special event.

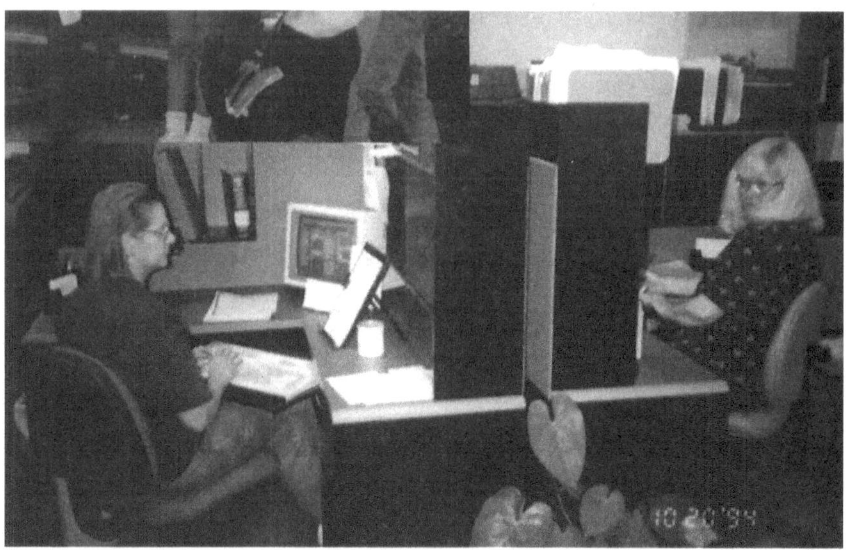

201. Billing clerks entering data at the accounting and insurance
office on Waverly Place (Cynthia Buist shown on right). The
clerks worked diligently to try to obtain the insurance revenues
due HCVAS.

202. In August 1994, HCVAS replaced the older trailer at the Canova Beach substation with a newer mobile home.

203. In September 1994, some of HCVAS' members posed for a photo shoot for the beachside consumer guide "The Magazine." The squad had 245 active volunteers who each donated on the average 41 hours per month. HCVAS now had to collect fees for its services due to changes in federal, state and county regulations.

204. Donnie and Lori Hughes and Jim and Sharon Irvin at a HCVAS
    awards banquet held at Sweetwaters on September 24, 1994.

205. HCVAS holding a joint training exercise with Melbourne and
    Palm Bay Fire Departments in October 1994.

206. Julie Holden speaking at an elementary school on Career Days
  in October 1994.

207. Mike Murphy and Ronnie Ferrell on a HCVAS special event at
  the TiCo Air Show. They're watching a Valliant Air Command
  DC-3 fly-by.

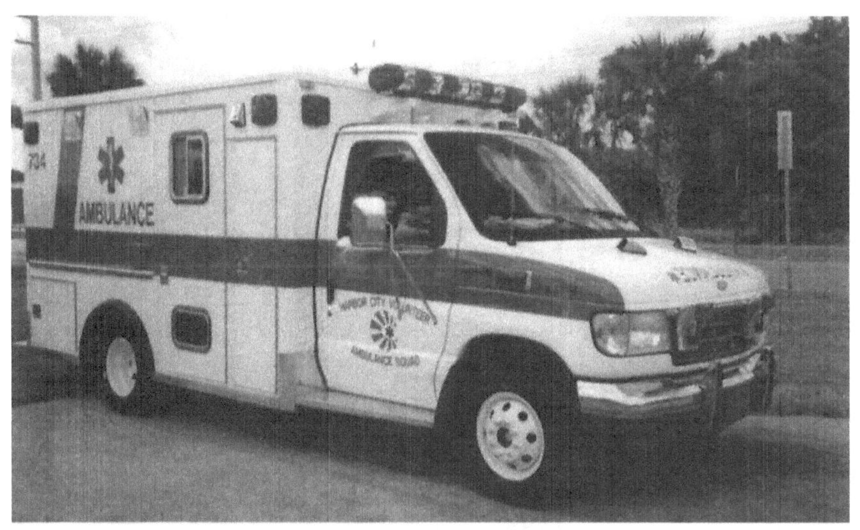

208. Unit 734, a new ambulance for Palm Bay substation on Clermont Street (1994). On November 15, the Board of County Commissioners voted to renew HCVAS' contract through September 30, 1999.

209. In December of 1994, employees voted on whether or not to join a union (IAEP: International Association of EMTs and Paramedics). In January 1995, the National Labor Relations Board (NLRB) impounded the union election ballots when management filed an appeal. Eventually, IAEP Local R5-70 was established at HCVAS.

210. Members and guests at a Christmas party held at Molly McGuires in Indian Harbor Beach (December 9, 1994).

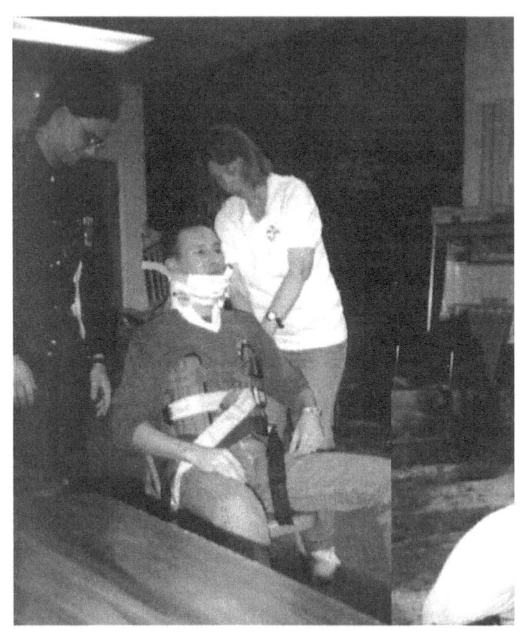

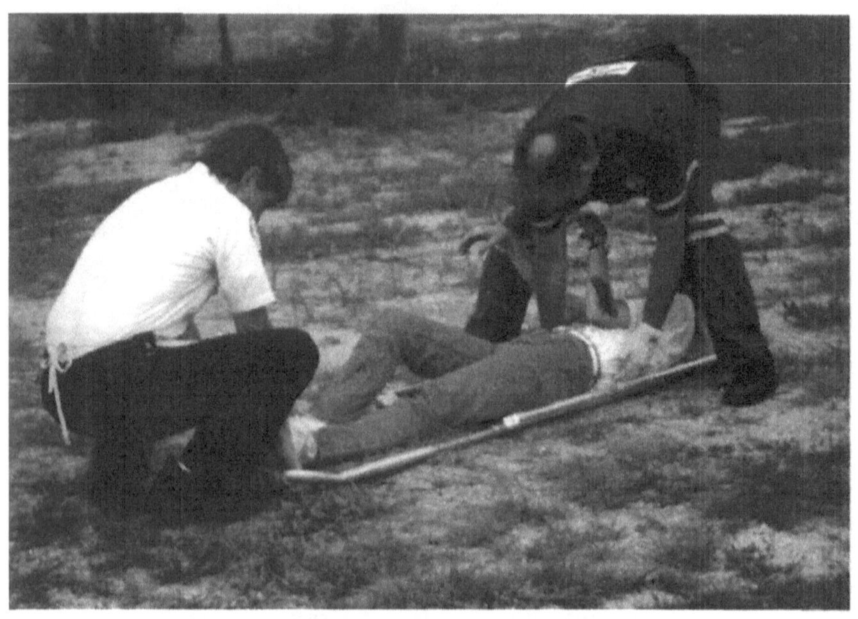

211. Sharon Irvin demonstrating the KED (a patient extrication device) in a rig training class and Jim Irvin with Melbourne firefighter Bobby Apel using the scoop on a "patient" in a MCI (mass casualty incident) drill. In 1995, HCVAS had 215 active volunteers who each donated an average of 31 hours per month. The squad responded to 20,840 ALS calls, 9,708 non-emergency calls, and 9,700 wheelchair calls.

212. In March 1995, Kevin Nelson, Mike Hunt, Cliff Roberts, Andy
     Eyster and Kerry Markey provided medical standby coverage for
     actor Danny Glover. He and his crew were making finishing
     touches to their movie *Dumbo Drop*.

213. In April 1995, Trooper Hultgreen was reunited with the HCVAS
     crew that had treated him (Dave Murtha, Lonnie Cantor, and
     Tim Byrd). The trooper had became ill and lost consciousness
     when tropical storm Gordon hit Snug Harbor and Barefoot Bay.
     The storm damaged over 500 homes on November 16, 1994.

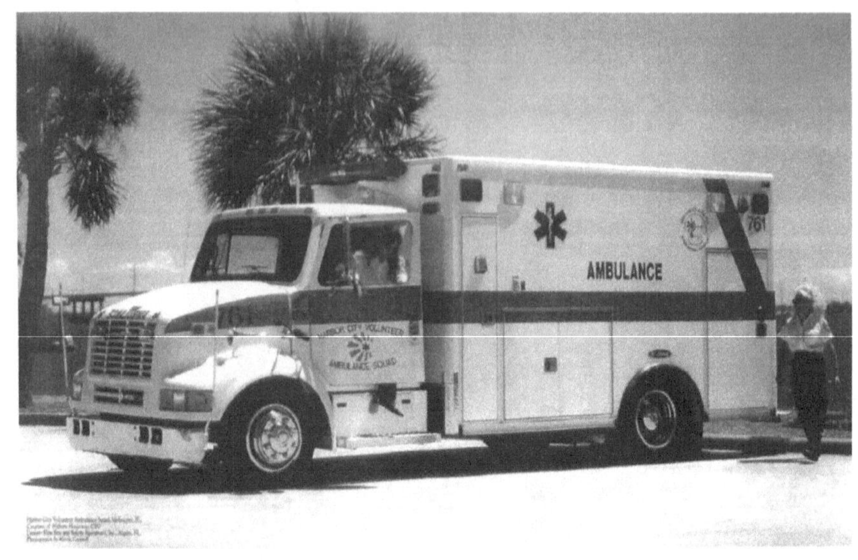

214. In May 1995, HCVAS approved a lease-purchase plan for six E-One vehicles: two BLS vans, two wheelchair vans, and two Street Warrior ambulances. Pictured is the squad's E-One Street Warrior Rescue that was featured in the "Emergency One 1997 Calendar" for the month of June.

215. Bobbi Kidd, HCVAS HR Director, shown with the ALS competition team (John Arnold, Dean White, Les Williams and Andy Eyster). In June 1995, the team competed at Jackson Memorial at the University of Miami and placed 2nd in the finals.

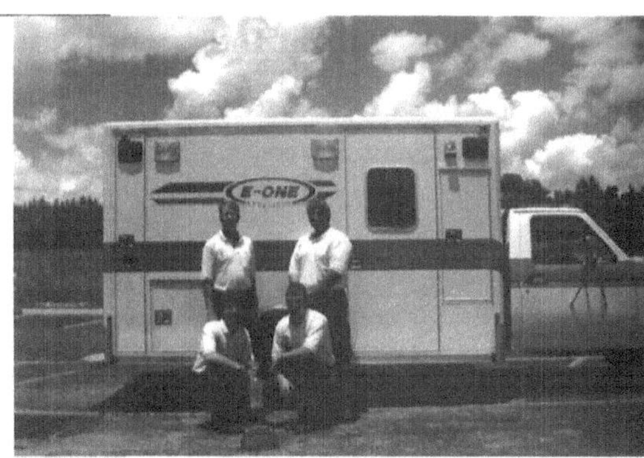

216. HCVAS' ALS competition team (back row: Les Williams and John Arnold; front row: Andy Eyster and Dean White). The team placed 1st at the Clincon competition in July 1995. Also shown is the uniform patch designed for the ALS team.

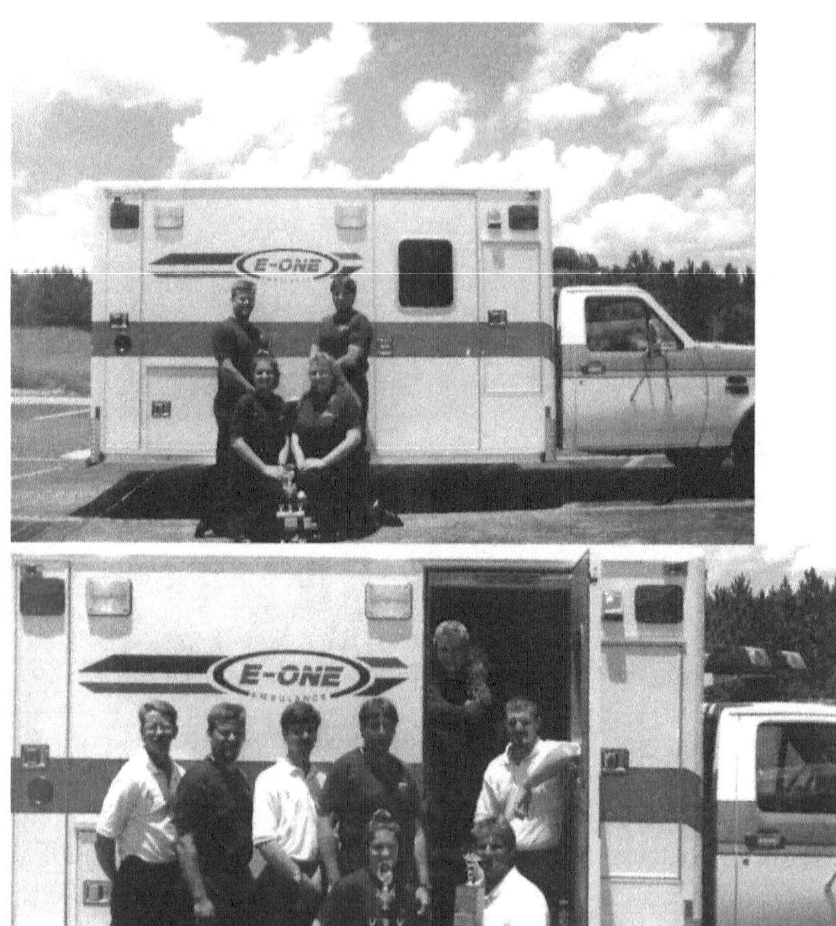

217. HCVAS' BLS competition team (back row: Shawn Riggan and Mike Strickland; front row: Liz Languell and Dawn Martin). The team also placed 1st at the Clincon competition in July 1995.

Also shown are both teams: (left to right) Les Williams, Shawn Riggan, Andy Eyster, Mike Strickland, Liz Languell, Dawn Martin, Dean White and John Arnold.

218. Celebrating the competition teams' 1st place victories at Clincon
are Bill Hoskovec and Bobbi Kidd (a) and Dr. Jerry Fitts,
HCVAS' Medical Director, and his wife (b).

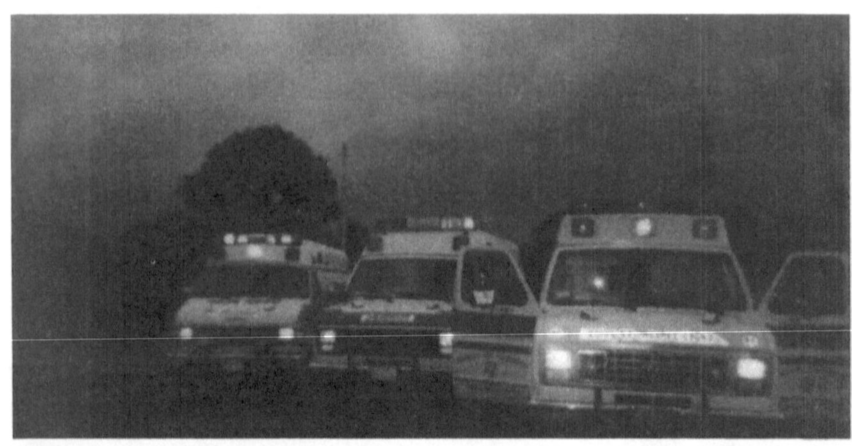

http://www.nhc.noaa.gov/1995erin.html

219. Shown are HCVAS' non-emergency transport units the night before Hurricane Erin hit Brevard County (July 31, 1995). On August 1, 1995, Hurricane Erin peeled back part of the roof at the Hickory Street headquarters, allowing rain to pour in. A command staff of 27 members set up temporary headquarters at HRMC.

220. Shown is some of the damage Hurricane Erin did to the Hickory Street headquarters and the insurance and accounting offices at Waverly Place.

221. The new HCVAS Operations center on Hibiscus Boulevard. The squad leased these facilities in August 1995 after Hurricane Erin damaged the Hickory Street headquarters. By the end of the year, HCVAS had lost over $500,000 in revenue for nonpayment of services. In 1996, the squad received an insurance settlement for damages that the hurricane caused to the Hickory Street headquarters.

222. In August 1995, HCVAS replaced the older trailer at the Palm Bay substation on Clermont Street with a newer mobile home.

223. Members and guests at a Christmas party held in December 1995 at the Tropics (formerly Molly McGuires) in Indian Harbor Beach.

The Times

Published by FLORIDA TODAY to serve Melbourne, Indialantic, Indian Harbour Beach, Melbourne Beach, Melbourne Village, Palm Shores, Satellite Beach, Suntree and West Melbourne

Volume 26, Number 23   Wednesday, July 24, 1996

Abels takes reins of ambulance squad

By VICKI DONNELLY
Times Correspondent

When it comes to the talents of Mike Abels, Palm Bay's loss is a gain for the rest of South Brevard County.

Abels, who resigned recently as the city manager of Palm Bay, will begin a new job as executive director of the Harbor City Volunteer Ambulance Squad next month.

"We are very happy to have Mike Abels with us now, and we're confident we have the right man to lead us into the 21st century," said Jim Wilson, a paramedic shift supervisor with the Harbor City Ambulance Squad. "Mike was selected from a pool of more than 100 applicants, and he stood out head and shoulders above the rest of the group. His experience is in the realm of being a visionary, and that's what we were hoping for in our next CEO."

The Harbor City Volunteer Ambulance Squad — celebrating it's 30th anniversary this year — covers South Brevard from Barnes Boulevard in Rockledge south to Valkaria Road, west to Osceola County and east to the ocean, Wilson said.

Approximately 100 employees work with about 200 volunteers at the ambulance squad to assure the best standards of care for the citizens of South Brevard.

Harbor City is, in fact, the second largest volunteer ambulance squad in the United States, with only one squad in Virginia showing more volunteers, Wilson said.

The Volunteer Ambulance Squad is funded through donations from individuals and companies, a and charges to the patients who are transported.

The ambulance squad covers calls ranging from the relatively minor (a child with a leg caught in the spokes of a bicycle) to the severe (plane, train and auto crashes, gun fights, etc.). What's important to remember, Wilson said, is that each call is traumatic — at least for the person who dialed 911.

"Most people don't realize that only a small percentage of the responses we go to are not true life emergencies," Wilson noted. "But it is an emergency to the people we respond to. The person who dials 911 is counting on us to come into the situation and take control of what they can't handle any longer."

Records show that Harbour City ambulances rolled 20,000 times during 1995.

The squad's main operations base is at 129 W. Hibiscus Boulevard in Melbourne, but there are additional stations throughout South Brevard, Wilson said. Three ambulance stations are located within the borders of Palm Bay.

Wilson and other ambulance squad employees and volunteers aren't the only ones looking forward to Aug. 9, when Abels will take the reins at Harbor City.

Sam Calabrese, acting chairman of Harbor City's board of directors, said Abels' qualifications couldn't come at a better time.

"His job is to run the company as efficiently and as profitably as possible," Calabrese said. "Palm Bay is going to suffer losing him. My reason for picking him is he can come here immediately and knows all the players. That's a plus for us."

224. In 1996, HCVAS hired Mike Abels as CEO and Alan Escoffery as chief financial officer (*The Times*, July 24, 1996). Escoffery's financial recovery plan and change to a billing process were approved because HCVAS now had outstanding accounts that exceeded $1.6 million. In December when Abels resigned to become Chief Administrative Officer for Sheriff Phil Williams, Escoffery became CEO.

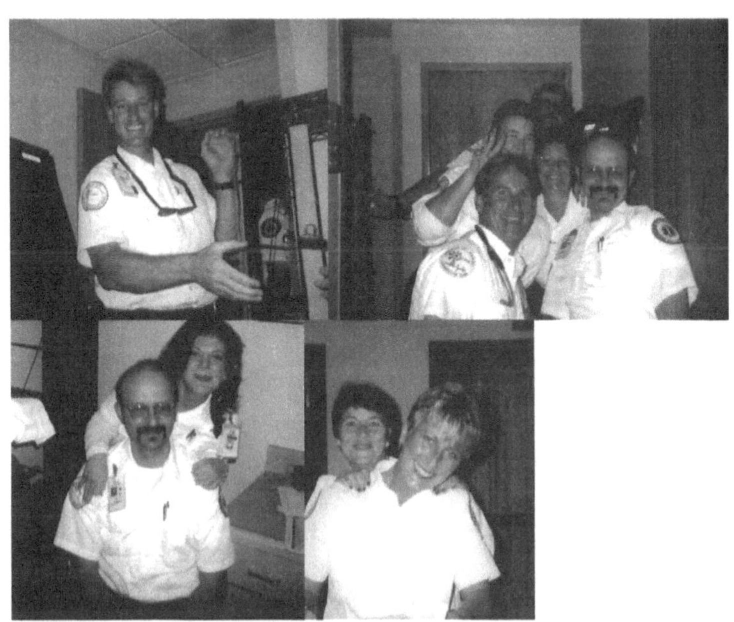

225. Some candid shots of members pulling duty. In 1996, HCVAS had 100 employees and 161 active volunteers who each donated on the average 35 hours per month. Field members now received yearly TB testing.

226. In October of 1996, HCVAS crew (from right to left: Dave Murtha, George Theofanous, Jim Wilson, and Bill Hoskovec) provided medical stand-by coverage for Vice President Gore at Wickham Park. Gore was campaigning for Cocoa Beach's John Byron, who was running for Congress.

227. HCVAS Honor Guard standing next to a Street Warrior ambulance decorated for the Christmas parade (1996). Shown are Randy Simmons, Kathy Blake, Talena King, Debbie Gaffney, James Clark, George Theofanous, Jackie Cote, and Scott Hartley. The honor guard participated in parades and at funerals.

228. Laddie Rutkowski, paramedic supervisor, talking on his cell phone (*Florida Today*, August 22, 1997). On July 7, 1997, the Medicare-Program Safeguards sent a letter to HCVAS, claiming it accepted payment for services in 1993 that were not appropriately documented or not medically necessary. HCVAS requested a medical hearing to appeal the claim that it was liable for an overpayment of $448,522.66. Medicare denied the request but accepted an extended repayment plan of 12 monthly payments of $40,166 each. HCVAS' Executive Board then approved the hiring of a lawyer experienced in Medicare appeal hearings.

229. On July 12, 1997, "Gathering of Friends and Family" held a fundraiser at Wickham Park for John DiBiasse, diagnosed with Leukemia. John, a paramedic with HCVAS for 10 years and then a nurse with HRMC, was undergoing chemotherapy. A number of HCVAS members had their heads shaved (shown are Jim Wilson, Marty Marsh, Les Williams, and Dave Segona) to match John's hair loss. More than 500 people attended the event, which raised over $18,000.

230. George Theofanous ("Theo") and Sue McCuiston posing with some of the equipment used on the ambulances. Members now had the option of wearing navy blue T-shirts instead of the standard white uniform shirts.

231. In 1997, HCVAS established an in-house maintenance and repair service at Lake Street in Melbourne and initiated a roving medical unit.

232. Teddy Bears donated by Target Stores for HCVAS ambulances. Crews gave the bears to comfort children transported to the hospital. In 1997, HCVAS lost $190,000 in non-receivable payment for its services. The majority (66%) of its services was given to Medicare beneficiaries, but up to 25% of the claims were denied. About 70% of HCVAS' budget was for employee salaries. The CEO proposed a Flexible Hours-System Status Management Plan to cut operating costs.

233. In 1997, the USAF converted PAFB hospital to an outpatient clinic. HCVAS then moved its Canova Beach substation to the fire station in PAFB South Housing, thus expanding its emergency service to include Patrick personnel and their families. This move gave the cash-strapped squad an additional source of revenue (*Florida Today*, August 27, 1997).

234. From early spring to the first week of July 1998, firestorms swept across Florida, causing $393 million in damages. When the fires subsided in Brevard County, they had burned 71,000 acres of mostly uninhabited land, 32 homes, and three businesses. Fortunately, no one was killed in the fires, and injuries were minor (*Florida Today*, August 2, 1998). The HCVAS crews that provided medical assistance to the firefighters were each given a coffee mug and a pass (shown) to the Disney World theme parks.

235. In July 1998, HCVAS relocated the Malabar substation (not shown) to a site near the Port Malabar Elementary School. The squad had 56 active volunteers who each donated on the average 35 hours per month. The CEO proposed dropping "volunteer" in HCVAS' name because 75% of personnel were employees.

236. On August 4, 1998, the Board of County Commissioners approved amendments to HCVAS' contract and provided funds for two new ambulances and staff for the county fire station on Murrell Road in Melbourne. In November, Medicare Part B Financial Services reimbursed HCVAS $328,434 for overpayments when it won its appeal. Yet, Medicare was denying 31% of HCVAS' claims as "not reasonable nor medically necessary," creating a potential $200,000 shortfall in the budget.

237. Substation on Aurora Road near Eau Gallie High School. In 1999, HCVAS replaced the older trailer with this newer mobile home.

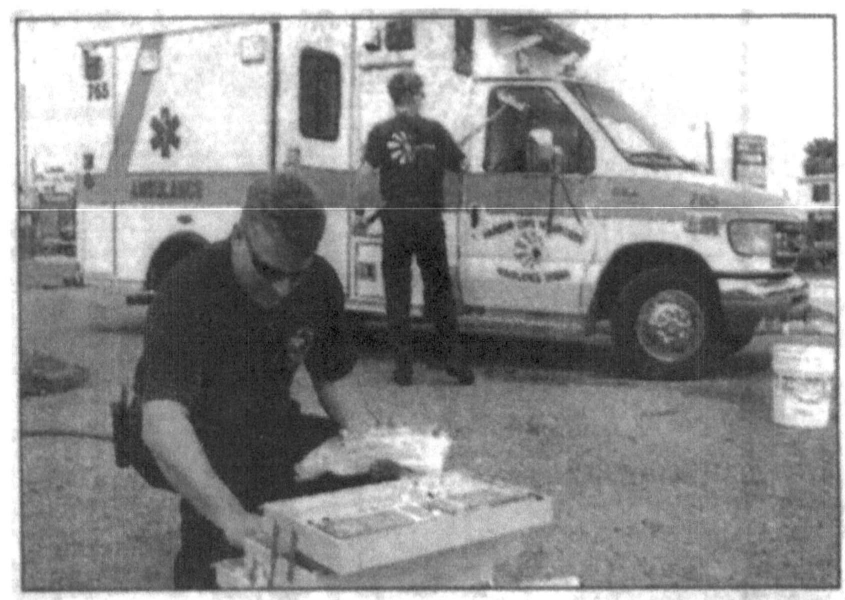

238. Dave Geer inspecting the drug box while Jeff Ayers washes the ambulance at the Eau Gallie substation (*Florida Today*, May 10, 1999). In January 1999, Bob Cunningham, former CEO of Coastal Health Systems, became the interim CEO for HCVAS. In March, the squad requested that the Board of County Commissioners extend its contract past September 30. It also submitted a proposal of $2.2 million for next year's budget, a $1 million increase over the previous year. In April, the commissioners rejected extending HCVAS' contract. They decided that consolidating EMS service for 23 municipalities made better sense for Brevard County. Therefore, HCVAS began the process of selling its assets and donating funds to scholarships and non-profit agencies.

239. Members posing for the camera in the last remaining days of the squad in September 1999. HCVAS had 151 employees (62 paramedics and 54 EMTs) and 36 active volunteers who each donated on the average 35 hours per month. Today, a number of the squad's employees work as fire-paramedics or in administrative positions for Brevard County. Others work in health-related fields (i.e. nurses, physician assistants, etc.), and some volunteer as ambulance attendants.

240. Members and guests at a "farewell" HCVAS picnic held September 30, 1999 at the BCC pavilion on Wickham Road, Melbourne.

241. At the farewell picnic, a tribute was given to the squad's (a) current field supervisors (Laddie Rutkowski, Mike Hunt, Matt Sands, Tim Dziak, and Sue McCuiston) and (b) former field supervisors.

242. On September 30, 1999, HCVAS "went out of service" after 33 years and turned over EMS coverage to Brevard County Fire/Rescue on October 1. The parade of ambulances with police escort ended at HCVAS' Operations center on Hibiscus Boulevard in Melbourne.

243. Members saying their good-byes after turning over the ambulances to Brevard County on October 1, 1999.

244. On October 24, 2000, Brevard Community College dedicated the Allied Health Center (Cocoa campus) to HCVAS. Along with dignitaries at the ribbon cutting ceremony were HCVAS members Thom Sousa (fourth from right) and Leo White (in uniform on right). When HCVAS went out of service, Leo White had accumulated over 36,000 volunteer hours. BCC has received over $600,000 from HCVAS to fund student scholarships, educational program enhancements, equipment purchases and an Endowed Faculty Chair (*Brevard Business News, Vol. 20 No. 2,* January 14, 2002).

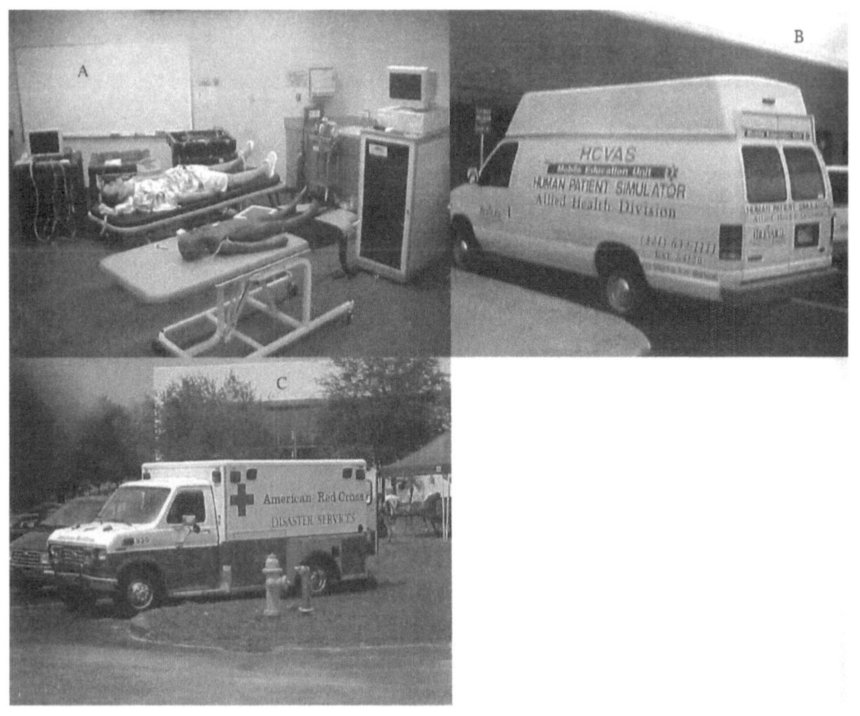

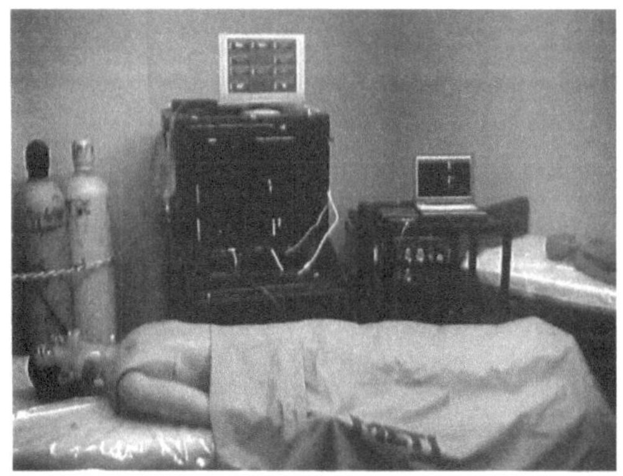

245. Some of HCVAS' assets have funded the following: (a) Human Patient Simulator for a lab in the Allied Health Building, BCC; (b) Allied Health van for the HCVAS Human Patient Simulator; (c) ambulance for the American Red Cross; and Human Patient Simulator for the Florida Medical Training Institute, Inc. in partnership with the School of Aeronautics, Florida Institute of Technology.

246. In March 2001, the City of Melbourne settled a year and one-half-old lawsuit with HCVAS, allowing it to sell the Hickory Street headquarters for $450,000. The city received $300,000. HCVAS received $150,000, which will fund scholarships for HCVAS members and donations to non-profit agencies in Brevard County (*Florida Today*, April 3, 2001).